ISBN-13: 978-1-59777-501-4
ISBN-10: 1-59777-501-0 $39.95 [US]

with Julie McCarron

Design by Sonia Fiore

LA GRANDE ODALISQUE BY JEAN AUGUSTE DOMINIQUE INGRES

Ladies of the Night

A Historical and Personal Perspective on the Oldest Profession in the World

Copyright © 2008 Simmons Books & Phoenix Books, Inc.

ISBN-10: 1-59777-501-0
ISBN-13: 978-1-59777-501-4
Library of Congress Cataloging-In-Publication Data Available

Book & Cover Design by: Sonia Fiore

Printed in the United States of America

Phoenix Books, Inc.
9465 Wilshire Boulevard, Suite 840
Beverly Hills, CA 90212

www.genesimmons.com
www.phoenixbooksandaudio.com

10 9 8 7 6 5 4 3 2 1

GENE SIMMONS

Ladies of the Night

A Historical and Personal Perspective on the Oldest Profession in the World

SIMMONS BOOKS & PHOENIX BOOKS
BEVERLY HILLS

Table of Contents

INTRODUCTION

The Dawn of Man

One day, at the dawn of our existence (about three to four million years ago) in a cave somewhere in the ice-cold regions of what was then Eastern Europe, the very first and very human female, Homo Erectus, turned to her male counterpart and grunted: "I'll stay in this nice, warm cave. YOU go out there in the freezing cold, risk your hairy ass, and bring me back some of that delicious Mastodon meat." *I'll trade you some of mine for some of yours.*

After that momentous event, nothing would ever be the same.

She discovered the enormous power she wields over him. Power that continues to rule the male of the species to this very day: his URGE TO MERGE.

And most astonishingly, this early female (though not as big, not as strong, and not nearly as fast as her male counterpart) nonetheless was able, in her own primitive way, to qualify, quantify and, most importantly, monetize her value!

There and then, the first profession was born. Before civilization. Before language. And before "cultural norms."

She figured out that she couldn't protect her mate from the dangers of the primitive world, or effectively hunt for food, either. Her value, she realized, was the children she could bear and the sex she could offer.

It warrants noting: he was probably already busy with other females in his own cave, as well as in other caves he happened upon as he followed and hunted the wandering herds.

"But that was then and this is now. Man has evolved."

You don't really believe that. Not really.

THE TRUTH—THE WHOLE TRUTH

Men don't think about reproducing; they think about sex. Men are simple: they work, eat, sleep, and have sex. Women think about reproducing, because they are biologically built for it. They have breasts and childbearing hips. Starting at the age of thirteen or so, their menstrual cycle reminds women every single month of their biological imperative to reproduce. Men are oblivious to reproduction for the sake of reproduction. All we have is the urge to have sex. And lots of it.

Women are (pardon me) biologically desperate, because they "drop" or produce only a few eggs per month. Men are never desperate; we produce hundreds of millions of sperm. A poor person carefully guards his two or four pennies, because that's all he has. A rich person with millions of dollars doesn't give a crap about a few pennies. The poor person wonders, "I don't know why he throws his money around like that." Because he has lots of it! To a rich person, those few little coins mean nothing; to a poor person, they are everything. A poor person who sees a dime rolling down the street grabs it—if it gets away, he'll never see that money ever again. A rich person just lets it roll by; he has more change than he knows what to do with.

This is the difference between men and women! Men are enormously rich, biologically speaking; women are very poor—again, biologically speaking. And you wonder why they can't talk with each other. Men and women are different animals. In essence, one is a meat-eater, the other is a vegetarian. The vegetarian asks, "What's all this about blood and meat, why can't you just eat leaves and grass?"

"How about I just eat *you*?" is the carnivore's answer.

These differences exist to this very day.

Social life in prehistoric times was all hunting, gathering and procreating. That's it. There's the biological argument of the original caveman coming home with the most amount of food who got to mate with the alpha female—perhaps the one with the biggest breasts (because men are visually stimulated). Strange, by the way, because big breasts signify to men that "I produce a great deal of milk and can nurture children," when in reality big breasts have nothing to do with this. The most flat-chested woman can feed four babies in a row, no problem. Big breasts are nothing more than a sexual come-on; there's no practical use for them. It's a biological trait that has evolved over time, because the male of the species started choosing the women with big breasts.

What attracted men way back then still holds true today— except, perhaps, in places like Brazil. That's why these days, given modern science, boob jobs are so popular. It's why European courtesans in Renaissance times wore corsets that pushed their boobs right up under their chins. For one reason only: to attract men. Men love big breasts.

The very first alpha females tended to be shapely, with hourglass figures. To this day, the generic hand movement in the air of a "figure eight" means the female form. To everyone all over the world this symbol immediately signifies "woman." Straight up and down doesn't say "woman" at all. In fact, the term "broad" (slang for a woman) comes from having broad hips.

If you examine some of the very first phallic symbols, scratched on cave walls the world over, they were males with huge phalluses, almost as big as their upper torsos. The earliest phallic art, either drawn or carved figurines, featured men with exaggeratedly large phalluses. The male with a very large penis, besides signifying pleasure, meant that he could sire the largest number of children. When again, that has nothing to do with virility. A guy with a tiny tool can still produce the most viable sperm and father plenty of children. However, he won't be picked first as the most desirable mate.

Likewise, the female with the biggest boobs and the curviest hips may not be able to bear children at all, but she'll draw the alpha male. A small, skinny, flat-chested woman may be very fertile, but she'll only get the run-offs of the men.

FRESCO IN POMPEII, between 89 BC and 79 AD

Sometimes called "Priapus with Caduceus" or nicknamed "Well-endowed Mercury" this fresco portrays the character Priapus walking away with the caduceus and wings of Mercury (supposedly). The joke was that Priapus has managed to steal from the god of all thieves as Mercury was known as the ultimate trickster. As for his extraordinarily large "piece"—that may have something to do with Priapus' being a god of fertility. Or perhaps his pride at having tricked Mercury went straight to his head!

Ladies of the Night

FRESCO FROM POMPEII

WARNING:
Do not read unless you are willing to accept the truth: that erotic art existed as far back as the destruction of the famous city of Pompeii!

Pompeii, the Roman city that suffered an untimely fate when Mount Vesuvius erupted in 79 AD, is the site of many considerably well-preserved artifacts. Of these, there is an abundance of art pieces and wall-carvings depicting sexually explicit scenes or anatomy. So why so much sex? There are several theories behind the pictures of men with impossibly large phalluses (one explanation is that they are signs of fertility, not meant to be erotic at all) and male and female intercourse (one explanation is that they were entryways to brothels in the area—either advertising the services of that particular business OR used as erotic "stimulus" for customers once inside the brothel). Whatever the reason, the erotic material of Pompeii can be compared to modern-day porn: it refuses to stay "buried." The Naples National Archaeological Museum even has a separate viewing room, intriguingly called "The Secret Cabinet," where all of the erotic art from Pompeii is housed.

GENE SIMMONS

"VENUS VON WILLENDORF," ca. 24,000-22,000 BC

This "Venus" statue was found in 1908 by an archaeologist at a Paleolithic site near Willendorf, Austria. Since the figure pre-dates the mythical goddess Venus, its name is based solely on her female figure. Because her feet have been barely developed, it is thought that the statue was designed to be held and not placed on a stand or simply looked at. From an artist's perspective, the figure seems to have been designed based on a woman looking down at her feet (hence, the large breasts and belly and shortened legs) or a pregnant woman (also perceived from above). The circular bands around her head have been speculated to be either rows of braided hair wrapped around the head or a headdress. Perhaps one of the oldest female figures in existence, "Venus" doesn't tell us much about the female figure that we don't already know.

Ladies of the Night

In recent excavations of Europe's largest prehistoric civilization, diggers unearthed a number of figurines, proving that women were dressing to impress eight thousand years ago! "Young women were beautifully dressed, like today's girls in short tops and miniskirts, and wore bracelets around their arms," the head archaeologist told the press.

Nothing has changed! Go to any party: women wear perfume, short skirts, high heels, push-up bras and lots of makeup. Because her power lies in attracting men! Sexually!

Interesting as all this may be, none of it goes to the heart of the matter, which is: the social structure in caveman days was all about killing everything, including other male rivals, to see who would be top dog.

Once the pecking order was established in early civilizations, men tended not to kill the females—at least not the ones who were useful (meaning they could provide him children, the next generation). Also, as the male got older, his offspring proved useful: they might support and protect him in his old age. The very first females figured their job out quickly.

There's a wonderful scene in the movie *QUEST FOR FIRE* in which a native girl happens to meet what appears to be a Neanderthal man. He's going to kill every animal and person in sight. When she sees that he is eating his meat, she wordlessly turns around and offers herself to him, in the way animals do. In the movie, the man is confused; he has never tried this position. Suddenly he gets the idea, mounts her from behind, and they have sex.

A man might think, "Now *that* is the ultimate liaison!"—with someone you never said a word to, someone whose name you never bothered to learn. It's a primordial coming together in urgency. There's the magic: circumventing civilization, before the female starts bothering herself and, more importantly, you with "What does this mean...? Where is all this going...?" Remember all that?

The most interesting part of this particular scene is that, after sex, the Neanderthal doesn't kill her. He is a killer, but he's discovered that this girl has a use. At the end of the scene, we see the native girl eating the meat that he killed. It's all just a deal. Quid pro quo. Without a word spoken.

In modern times, some women get married. Some women date. Call it what you will: there is always a price...for the male.

Today, when the male of the species takes a female out on a date, he will pay. He always has. He always will. When a fifteen-year-old kid takes a girl to the movies, hoping for nothing more than a kiss at the end of the evening...he will pay. In every culture on the face of the planet, the male always pays.

Men might ask, "Do you love me?" Women might ask, "How MUCH do you love me?"

HARMONY before MATRIMONY.

HARMONY BEFORE MATRIMONY, *James Gillray, 1805*

A cautionary tale about the hazards of holy matrimony, this piece shows how happy a couple is *before* marriage (as the title suggests). Gillray, the artist, published a piece not long afterwards that showed the same couple *after* marriage. The results: not so harmonious.

Marriage and Monogamy

In scientific terms, the word "marriage" means a "durable connection between male and female, lasting beyond a mere act of propagation, till after the birth of the offspring."

But the reality of the animal kingdom, incidentally, is that there are almost NO (as in none...zero) monogamous animals—only three percent of mammals and fifteen percent of primates. These figures include females as well. Here's why: The female has to make sure that she gets the best sperm from the healthiest male, to ensure healthy and strong offspring. The male has to make sure that he impregnates as many females as he can, to ensure that his line doesn't die with him.

Americans take it for granted that marriage is a spiritual AND legal binding of one man and one woman for life. The truth of the matter is that in many societies all over the world, marriage often consisted of one male and his wives (plural). Just read the Old Testament or the Koran, where there are numerous examples of men with more than one wife.

Polygamy is the practice of marriage to more than one spouse—by either sex. Polyandry is when a woman has more than one husband—a rare phenomenon. Polygyny, when a man has more than one wife, is much more common, even now. Modern-day Africa is a good example. In the second-largest continent on earth, with its population of more than 900 million people, one man/many wives is a common scenario. In countries south of the Sahara, approximately half of all women live in polygynous households. In West Africa, Central Africa, and East Africa, these percentages are approximately one-fourth to one-third of all women.

In America, polygyny was practiced by the early Mormons, but was officially outlawed in 1890, though a few fundamentalist sects still have multiple wives today. The modern American ideal of marriage is very traditional: one man, one wife, for life.

Which makes statistics concerning infidelity difficult to verify, since one would assume many men are reluctant to admit to indiscretions. However, by some estimates (CNN), man wanders during marriage to the tune of sixty to seventy percent of the time. And marriages end in divorce within a few years, fifty to sixty percent of the time.

CHAPTER ONE
My Thoughts on Ladies

*B*efore we begin this fun-filled, personal and historical overview of the world's oldest profession, let's lay down some ground rules.

I love women. Period.

Almost all men do.

Somewhere between that feeling and the real world lies "the price" for loving women.

It's said that women have sex for the MEANING. Men have sex for the FEELING.

If you love and respect women, and I do, then I believe her choices for herself—including her own sexuality and how she chooses to make money—are her own business. Whether the two intertwine in marriage or not is up to her. Whatever decision she makes for herself is something I want to support. I am not here to judge women's personal choices or how they choose to empower themselves.

And maybe that's what this is really all about.

In this book, we are talking about consenting adults entering into a mutually satisfactory agreement. Nobody gets hurt, nobody is under duress, and nobody is doing anything against his *or* her own free will. This book is not about the dark side of prostitution— and there is a very dark side to the world's oldest profession. There is a dark side to most institutions.

The tone of this book is going to be light in nature. With a sense of humor, if you will. I neither condone nor condemn the Ladies. In point of fact, they will not be referred to as prostitutes, whores or other derogatory references. The lower end of the "Ladies of the Night Society" certainly teems with the part of the profession usually disparaged in literature. But the higher end of that profession, then and now, is populated with Ladies who approach their profession with style and, yes, grace: from the courtesans of Europe's Renaissance period to Japan's geishas and even to today's Park Avenue Ladies. The majordomo of a house of ill repute is referred to as a Madam, or Madame. And it is in that light that we prefer to cast our gaze.

The Ladies themselves seem to have a sense of humor about all this. They always know what the transaction is about: Money. So does, one would presume, their customer. It is my contention that society veils the man/woman relationship and judges certain monetary exchanges "Romantic," while outright cash payments are "Prostitution."

My question is, what's the difference?

One way or the other, man will pay. He always has. And, he seems ready, willing and eager to do so: on first dates with his girlfriend; before, during and after marriage; in almost all facets of the male/female relationship.

There are differences, however, in how society views the "monetary exchange." And it is in that area that I take exception to the hypocrisy of it all.

Though I've said it before, I am reminded of the notion that a Lady of the Night will always tell you before "the encounter" (in business, it's usually referred to as "full disclosure before the fact") how much she wants to get paid for services performed. She will also be clear with you that it's strictly sex. She's not looking for a relationship or marriage. She just wants to get paid.

Now, a man's potential wife will usually shy away from discussions having to do with compensation (money). If he, the potential husband, asks his beloved, soon-to-be wife: "Sweetheart, before we get married…and, if, perchance, one day we get divorced—and statistics tell us it's almost bound to happen—how much money are you expecting from me?"

She will either tell it straight—that as the law of the land dictates, she will expect to get half of his gross, pre-tax dollars, plus all the jewelry he bought her, the insurance he paid for, and so on—or she will cry and say, "That's so unromantic."

I would venture to say that she will cry and choose the latter.

And he will usually cave. And marry her. And (probably) pay the consequences later. Yes, I know. Some women make more money than men. But stay with me, please.

And now the upsetting part (for women): The Lady of the Night (remember her?) will, in the grand tradition of ethical, upfront behavior, tell you *before the fact* what the deal is.

A man's beloved potential future wife might only tell him after the fact what the deal is.

Which one is more ethical?

LET'S BE BRUTALLY HONEST FOR A MOMENT

My contention is that society should not have the power to decide who and what you are or how you earn a living. I'm not here to sit as judge and jury just because a woman chooses to trade sexual favors for money, in whatever form that may take— wife, mistress, or Lady of the Night.

Yes, I believe in love. I also believe a woman loves a man more if he can support himself and his family. Even in a world where women can earn their own money, his "value" is still wrapped up in his earning ability.

He pulls up in a garbage truck and asks her for a date. Or, the same guy pulls up in a Rolls and asks her for a date. Who's she going to choose?

She pulls up in a garbage truck, or a Rolls-Royce. Men don't care. As long as she's hot.

You know it, and I know it.

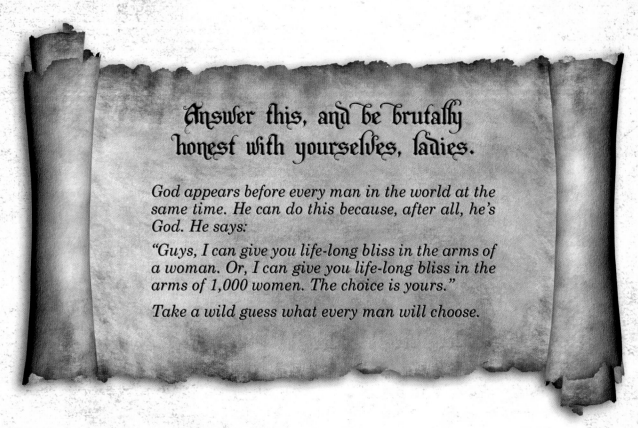

Answer this, and be brutally honest with yourselves, ladies.

God appears before every man in the world at the same time. He can do this because, after all, he's God. He says:

"Guys, I can give you life-long bliss in the arms of a woman. Or, I can give you life-long bliss in the arms of 1,000 women. The choice is yours."

Take a wild guess what every man will choose.

Since women instinctively know every man's answer to the above, we should never have to engage in a dialogue regarding the differences between the male and the female of the species, ever again. And therefore, my guess is that in good times and in bad times, Ladies of the Night will always do well. There's never a recession in that field of work. Well, after he's happy there is a kind of "recession"....

The business of sex always does well. It always has... everywhere. Because half the planet is populated by men, and men are happy to pay for it.

Show me the happiest married man with the prettiest, sweetest wife imaginable and I'll show you a man who may be tempted by a Lady of the Night (or mistress) and eventually have an affair. (That's what CNN tells us, by the way.) This concept is what tortures women every day of their lives. They talk about it endlessly on *Oprah, Ellen* and *Martha* (none of whom, I might add, are married—they must know something!).

Women don't much like Ladies of the Night. Not much at all.

They don't like that a woman can be upfront and want to charge money for sex—though one might argue there is certainly a price to pay for marriage (before, during and after). Mostly they don't like that there are women out there who will always make it easier for a man to get what he wants. He won't have to buy her for a lifetime. He can just rent her for a night.

And that alternative is a threat to most of the women in the world.

A threat to her. An alternative for him. Kindly remind yourself that actor Hugh Grant was caught with a Hollywood "Lady of the Night" while he was with actress Elizabeth Hurley.

THE TRUTH

The Blessed Union has finally taken place!

He has found his soul mate. His life partner. The woman he loves!

And as they descend the stairs of the church/temple where they just took their holy vows, and their adoring friends, family and well-wishers throw rice to wish them lifelong happiness, and as he lovingly stares into the beautiful eyes of his new wife and tenderly kisses her…when he raises his head back up and looks around, he catches a glimpse out of the corner of his eye…over there…to his right.

And there she stands.

She is clearly out of place at a wedding. Her plunging neckline reveals two heaving, well-packed and well-placed melons. She is staring directly at him, parting her moist, red lips and letting him know in no uncertain terms that she is available…to him!

Ladies, what is the first thought that crosses your beloved's mind?

That's why the oldest profession will exist forever. Because there are men.

Now ladies, lest you think you only have to worry about other women out there who are more beautiful and desirable than you are, that's not your only problem. To a man (fortunately or unfortunately, depending on your point of view) the most beautiful woman is the closest one. Not always, but often enough for you to privately mutter to yourself, "Ain't that the truth!"

Or, as the joke goes, men are cursed and blessed with a classic syndrome. It's called "2 at 10 and 10 at 2." It goes something like this....

He goes into a bar. It's 10 p.m. Over in the corner, a not-too-attractive woman smiles at him. She's a 2.

But at 2 a.m., she's a 10!

If a woman should have a choice regarding how she leads her life, in love and in sex, so should a man. Get married if you want to. If you don't want to, don't.

And what a man wants for himself really, ultimately has nothing to do with you, ladies. It's actually (pardon my bluntness) none of your business.

Right about now, the women are thinking, "But I don't WANT him to want what he wants for himself. I want him to want ME!"

That's biology talking. And the same biological imperative that tortures women to land a husband during her child-bearing years is the same biological imperative that tortures men to "hunt" for as many women as he can for the rest of his life! Bluntly speaking.

Women have been trying to figure out why men are the way they are. Forever.

Men, on the other hand, have never tried to figure out what makes women tick. You want marriage and babies. You

Ladies of the Night

want to go shopping. You want a career. Fine. Great. None of this is even in a man's mindset.

Men don't sit around and wonder, "Where is this going? Why hasn't she called me? Do I have my mother's hips?"

Men don't read *Cosmo* articles like "10 Ways to Keep Her Happy." That's because we are always and ultimately concerned with…ourselves!

Ouch! Send your hate mail to: _____

There are happy marriages where both the man and woman remain sexually faithful to each other and never wander, believe it or not. Though I would venture to say in some of these cases religion plays a very important role—the shared strong conviction that God's wrath will descend upon all adulterers, because (here we go again) the tendency for men is to wander.

The tone of this book will strike you as humorous and well-intentioned, I hope. Really.

I prefer to use the word LADIES. I am not fond of the words prostitute, whore or wife. (Again, send your hate mail to….) I'm not fond of labels of any kind. Whatever you want for yourself should be your own personal definition of your happiness.

And let's remember! ALL women are ladies. From the very first cavewoman, to the brothels of Rome, the geishas of Japan, the courtesans of Europe's Renaissance period…even to today's late-night secret telephone number that gets dialed when his "urge" strikes.

They're the Ladies of the Night.

Some Good Advice

LADIES: If you want to get married, be someone's mistress, work as a call girl, or just have all the fun you want with whomever you like, those are your choices to make for yourself. Not his, or society's. Whether you're married or single, figure out what you want to do with your life, do it, and let society be damned. Let the cards fall where they may. The cards are men, and trust me, they will continue to do what they've done since the dawn of civilization. That means: desire women. All sorts of women. All the time.

Men can't put a lock on their equipment. Women have forever tried to keep "their things" under control, but it's never worked. Men tend to do what they want to do. A woman's choices are to either be tortured by her man's lack of total commitment, or decide to empower herself.

This is not to say I encourage women to become Ladies of the Night. Far from it. I am simply pointing out that women may as well monetize their God-given "assets."

It's worth noting, throughout history, women have never had access to power. Women have never had the right to voice their opinions on almost any topic—politics, business, religion—at least until very recently, and then haltingly, at best. All those doors were closed to her. About the only thing women have ever owned (and even that can be debated) is their own bodies. And their sexuality.

Given the above, shouldn't a woman once and for all be the sole decision-maker regarding how and when she wants to use her "assets"? Her body. Her sex.

Not public opinion.

Not even the scorn of other women.

Women, perhaps unconsciously, often say the words, "I'm worth it." As in, MONEY.

Guys, you try saying that and see what the results are. Zero.

Woman won't pay for it. Man will. Simple as that.

The eternal cat and mouse game has existed since we crawled out of the ooze we were both created in, and it will continue to go on. The mouse wants the cheese. The cat wants only the mouse. The cat wants to do to the mouse what the mouse wants to do to the cheese: eat it. And swallow.

So ladies, if you haven't gotten a thick skin by now, or developed a sense of humor about the whole thing, might I suggest a hypothetical? It goes like this:

An old couple has been married for fifty or more years. Irving is ninety-two, Magda is in her late seventies. They are at a dance for old people—you've got to keep moving when you get to that age, or everything stops. A friend pokes Irving's side and says, "Hey Irving…your wife Magda's playing around a little bit tonight…look at her…she's flirting with that guy!"

Ninety-two-year-old Irving turns to his friend and replies, "I feel soooo good today. I had such a good crap!"

See, when you're ninety-two years old, the only thing you care about is being regular. You won't give a damn if she—or he—is flirting with anybody. You'll be in a coffin next week…what do you care what all this means? All the worries, fears, concerns that women have for most of their lives…it's only because you still have a long life ahead of you. When you're eighty-five or ninety years old, you won't care a bit. You'll care about your health and your children and enjoying the last bit of time you have alive.

If you'll just take the old people's perspective—"Don't bug me too much, don't make a lot of noise, and just let me be regular"—you'll be fine. The folly of youth guarantees that the younger you are, the stupider you are. This is why girls get into catfights, guys kill each other over a girlfriend…. That's biology and youth. The older you get, the more mature you become and the quicker you get over things. You learn to just shrug your shoulders about a lot of things.

Remember, it all ultimately comes down to poop.

CHAPTER TWO

A Word About the

Earliest Civilizations

*T*he earliest *written* accounts of sex appeared not on cave walls, but on clay tablets from the ancient civilization of Mesopotamia, which reached its zenith more than 3000 years BC. A group of diverse, independent city-states located between the Tigris and Euphrates rivers in an area known as the Fertile Crescent, Mesopotamia is widely considered to be the cradle of civilization.

Mesopotamia was a patriarchal class society, a system in which women were subservient to men. According to what we've learned from these tablets, marital sex for Mesopotamians was not a moral issue but simply a one-sided business arrangement. The woman's body was the property of her husband, especially its reproductive capacity. Adultery would be judged a crime against a woman's husband, in that she was depriving her husband of his exclusive sexual access; her lover's crime was in effect one of theft.

Certainly there was no expectation that the husband would be completely faithful to his wife. Men had easy access to all the household slaves for sexual purposes, or they could visit prostitutes with no social stigma attached to the act.

The ancient kings in some Mesopotamian cities had actual performance clauses in their contracts! Between 2100 and 1600 BC it was a king's sacred duty to have sexual intercourse with a priestess or other exalted woman at a temple who represented Ishtar, the goddess of sexual activity. The king complied with this rite to ensure a successful year—not only in terms of fertility, but also in battle. Temple priestesses, or prostitutes, were living symbols of the Mesopotamians' belief in the strong, healing power of sex and acceptance of Ladies of the Night.

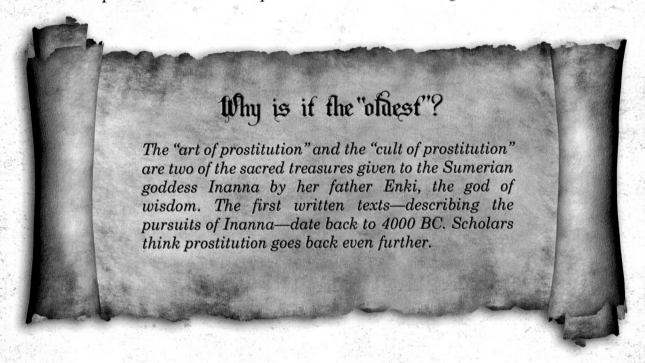

Why is it the "oldest"?

The "art of prostitution" and the "cult of prostitution" are two of the sacred treasures given to the Sumerian goddess Inanna by her father Enki, the god of wisdom. The first written texts—describing the pursuits of Inanna—date back to 4000 BC. Scholars think prostitution goes back even further.

The epic tale *Gilgamesh* mentions the goddess Ishtar for the first time in recorded literature. It also tells another story about a powerful Lady of the Night. The hero Gilgamesh must subdue Incadoo, a mighty beast-like creature. Gilgamesh reasons that the flesh is mightier than the sword and decides not to face the monster in hand-to-hand combat. He decides that the better, easier way to capture this wild man is to send him a prostitute who will seduce him. And that is just what she does—Incadoo

Ladies of the Night

and the Lady have intercourse for six straight days and seven nights. Incadoo is so weakened by his week-long fling that he becomes civilized without putting up a fight. This is certainly the first recorded case of sex—and a Lady—soothing the savage beast.

BABYLONIAN MARRIAGE MARKET, *Edwin Long, 1875*

Set many years after the flourishing of ancient Mesopotamia, this famous painting by British artist Edwin Long depicts the Babylonian marriage market where women were sold to prospective husbands. Babylon was one of the most important cities of the Mesopotamian region, in the Middle East near the Euphrates River. In 689 BC, the city was destroyed by its enemies, the Assyrians, although it was rebuilt and became legendary for its beautiful and luxurious architecture—and women, too!

The Very First Lady of the Night

Ishtar, the goddess of sexual activity and fertility, was a dangerous and volatile deity. Besides being the goddess of love in ancient Sumeria (Babylon), she was also a goddess of war. The patron of all prostitutes, including lowly women who sold their bodies in doorways and behind taverns, she herself cared more for love than money: she willingly had sex with any man she desired.

Ishtar is immortalized as the very first prostitute in literature, the epic Gilgamesh about the adventures of a virile prince, which dates back to nearly 2000 BC. She was known by many names over time, including The Great Whore of Babylon, Heavenly Prostitute, and Mother of Harlots. She was familiarly called HAR and HORA, which is where the words "harlot" and "whore" come from. Ancient sculptures of Ishtar often depict her sitting in a window, waiting for customers; or in a characteristic breast-offering pose.

ISHTAR'S FAMOUS
"BREAST-OFFERING" POSE,
*a sales tactic used by
modern Ladies as well.*

*This carving depicts the first **HORA** in history. Besides being the Babylonian goddess of love, she was the goddess of war—makes sense, really.*

THE APOCALYPSE: THE WOMAN OF BABYLON, Albrecht Durer, (1496-8)

This woodcut from the famous German artist Albrecht Durer shows The Whore of Babylon, who is described in the Bible as having written upon her forehead: "MYSTERY, BABYLON THE GREAT, THE MOTHER OF HARLOTS AND ABOMINATIONS OF THE EARTH." Dangerous and volatile, sexy and fertile, she was the first Lady of the Night.

Marriage—Who Started This Institution?

We can trace many aspects of the modern marriage all the way back to ancient Mesopotamia—specifically Babylonia, where concepts such as the wedding ceremony, marriage, and divorce were developed. Surviving documents of the time include legal papers that demonstrate how marital relationships started with a proposal, were followed by an official marriage contract, and ended with a wedding.

In terms of the ceremony, the wife was "delivered" to the husband. The couple would then recite vows in front of witnesses, which could be summed up essentially as the man publicly affirming: "She is my wife." During the ceremony of betrothal (meaning "truth" ceremony), the husband poured perfume on the head of his wife and gave her presents. Presents, money, and wealth have always played a large part in marriage.

In Mesopotamia, the suitor and father of the bride decided on her price beforehand, and the bride received that money upon their marriage day. If a woman's husband-to-be died before the actual marriage ceremony, she got her pick of his brothers. If the prospective bride died, her intended got to pick another wife from her sisters. Historical records prove that ancestral family names existed and were used for identification purposes, just like our last names today. What has changed is that the prospective bride back then had no say in any of the decisions.

As fertility was the paramount concern in Mesopotamian times, men were allowed to "bed hop" if their wives were infertile. In such cases, a man might choose to take on a concubine in addition to his wife. This right, which the Code of Hammurabi granted to the Babylonians, remained in force for nearly five hundred years. It did not, however, permit the husband to have two "wives"; this title belonged to the legal wife alone, from the moment her husband placed the veil upon her during their wedding ceremony.

Perhaps not much has changed, after all. In Western society, men marry women (though this is a declining phenomenon) and often have mistresses or "outside liasions." But only the "wife" maintains the official title...and control of ALL decision-making (before, during and after the marriage, for as long as they both shall live).

Which perhaps brings us to the age-old joke: Why do men die younger than their wives? Because they want to.

CHAPTER THREE

Ladies of Ancient Greece

Ancient Greece was a flourishing society 2,500 years ago. It was a land where free thinking was ardently encouraged—whether the topic be religion, history or sex. Today we tend to view the ancient Greeks as sexually liberated people; they were certainly not as hung up on sexual matters as we are today. Sex, of any variety, was simply a natural part of life to them.

It may have all started with their gods and goddesses: Aphrodite was the goddess of love, beauty and sexual rapture, and the almighty Zeus was a philandering husband who ravished goddesses, mortal women and young boys alike. Other creatures from Greek mythology, such as half-man/half-goat Pan, represented the more carnal, animal impulses of sexual behavior: randy and insatiable.

ILLUSTRATION FROM "STORIES FROM THE GREEK TRAGEDIANS"
by Alfred John Church, 1879

Zeus is perhaps the most infamous character in ancient Greek mythology: the god of all gods. Zeus had over three dozen women, with each of whom he had at least one (and often upwards of three) children. To say he was the most virile man in mythology would not be an exaggeration. Perhaps it was his gigantic...thunderbolt.

Unlike most societies of the western world, the Greeks attached no stigma to prostitution. They saw sexual activity as essential to healthy vitality. Romantic love between mortal Greek men and women was rare; Greek marriages were business arrangements set up to carefully ensure bloodlines and inheritances. Greek men routinely sought sexual pleasure outside the marriage bed. Their wives tended to be ten to twenty years younger than their spouses (sounds similar to the modern age!) as men were not allowed to marry before the age of thirty. Wives were expected to tend to matters of hearth and home and were generally regarded as little more than chattel, suitable only for raising families. Their husbands, meanwhile, were free to satisfy their desires how and where they pleased.

They had plenty of options. Athens was a prominent commercial city where streetwalkers openly plied their trade on the city streets. These women represented the lowest rung of the sexual hierarchy, and were known as *pornae*—the root word from

Ladies of the Night

which the English word pornography is derived. Visiting one of these street prostitutes was quick, inexpensive, and when the sex act was over, so was the relationship. Pornae advertised their services by engraving words and symbols on the soles of their sandals, leaving a path in the dusty streets for customers to follow. Very inventive, if you ask me. Incidentally, advertising and branding are still the cornerstone of any business!

A COURTESAN TIES UP HER DRESS WHILE HER CLIENT WATCHES
ancient Greek Pottery, ca. 490

This musician/prostitute is in the upper echelons of ancient Greek Ladies. Women like her often had clever business tactics to attract customers. They wore makeup to look more attractive, and their sandals left imprints in the grounds that read "Follow me." Ingenious!

COURTESAN MASK OR PSEUDOKORE, 3rd-2nd centuries BC

In Greek literature, prostitutes were the celebrities of the time, starring in many a New Comedy (it was out with the Old Comedy and in with the new, apparently). Of course, it's easy to see the parallels in our current film industry....

In one play by Aristophanes, entitled *Assemblywomen*, the "regular" women of the town get so jealous of the prostitutes—and their experienced ways—that they ban the "tricked-out" Ladies from the city! Ovid and Plato have also both written plays starring the ever-popular prostitute. Greek literature has somehow remained timely and relevant no matter how far our society advances.

The upscale sisters to the pornae were the *hetaerae*, meaning companion. These women moved in the upper social strata of Greek society. Many were former slaves who had become skilled enough in the art of lovemaking and pleasing men to buy their own freedom and set themselves up in a profitable business. The hetaerae entertained the husbands at lavish symposiums, while the dutiful Greek wives stayed safely at home. A popular door prize was that the winner of a raffle could take the girl (or boy) of their choice home for the night.

Ladies of the Night

Hetaerae captured the imaginations of poets and playwrights and artists of the time. Widely considered the most beautiful women of Greece, a hetaera is rumored to be the inspiration behind Botticelli's most famous painting of Venus emerging from the sea. Even the great scholar and philosopher Socrates admired their beauty, saying of one particularly gorgeous hetaera that her beauty must be seen in person to be believed; no words could do her justice.

BIRTH OF VENUS, Sandro Botticelli, ca. 1485

Botticelli's most famous painting may have been inspired by the ancient Greek prostitutes. This pagan work emphasizes the naked female figure. In addition, the sea shell from which she emerges was a metaphor for a woman's vulva.

GENE SIMMONS

HETAERA URINATING INTO A SKYPHOS, ancient Greek pottery, ca. 480 BC

In ancient Greece, the hetaerae were courtesans. This is one of those courtesans in a compromised position! The word hetaerae literally means "companions" and these women were held in a higher esteem than the average prostitute.

Greek pottery often depicted the "daily life" of people at the time. Grouped into four categories, the activities of "daily life" depicted are: banquet scenes, sexual activities, toilet scenes, and scenes of slavery/punishment. Prostitutes commonly found in the toilet scenes had less-than-perfect bodies. Perhaps this is where toilet humor originated?

Ladies of the Night

The vast majority of Greek men patronized prostitutes but at the same time blamed their wives for being oversexed! The ancient Greeks believed that women were more sexually driven than men. As they demanded complete sexual fidelity from their wives, and female adultery was punishable by death, how did Greek women receive sexual satisfaction? From dildoes. Yes, women were pleasuring themselves with crude dildoes more than 2,500 years ago.

Meanwhile, their husbands enjoyed every possible distraction. Greek households were divided by gender into two halves: the men's and the women's quarters. The great hall where parties were held was located in the men's section; this is where prominent men entertained and hosted private parties and orgies.

Wives were not welcome, as among the attendees at these parties were the high-end call girls of the day, who were called "servants of Aphrodite." These professionals were the most liberated women in Greek society. They publicly socialized with their male companions and were free to attend banquets and other social events with their lovers. They were witty, cultivated and highly desirable (and expensive) company.

The actual Servants of Aphrodite were the sacred prostitutes of Corinth, the Greek port city that was known as the "Amsterdam of the ancient world." Tired sailors returning to port would stagger up more than a thousand steps to the Acrocorinth to visit the Temple of Aphrodite. It was said that more than a thousand beautiful women in incense-filled, candlelit confines worked around the clock gathering funds for their deity. Visitors believed that sexual intercourse with one of Aphrodite's servants offered a mystical union with the goddess herself—uninhibited pagans coupling in ecstasy before her statue in the perpetual twilight of the temple. Accordingly, ship captains would spend fortunes there, and an old proverb says: "The voyage to Corinth isn't for just any man."

The reality may not have lived up to the myth—in fact, Aphrodite's servants, who may or may not have been attractive, were not always willing volunteers. Corinth's many cosmopolitan pornae were slaves purchased by wealthy Greeks and dedicated to the temple as a form of religious offering. (Once, a victorious athlete at the Olympic Games donated 100 women in a lump sum.) Also, recent excavations at the Corinth fortress have found the temple too small for 100 women to be working, let alone 1,000, so few—if any—carnal rites were literally conducted at the goddess' feet.

It is more likely that sex slaves received their clients in makeshift brothels around the temple, huddling with their customers on lumpy straw mattresses in small, dark, airless stalls, with crude illustrations painted above the booths demonstrating each girl's specialty. It is true that Aphrodite was the patron goddess of Corinth, and that the working Ladies there felt they had a special relationship with her—but this reverence didn't do them much practical good.

Demosthenes, a prominent Greek statesman, proclaimed in front of an assembly of citizens, "We have courtesans for pleasure, concubines to provide for our daily needs, and our spouses to give us legitimate children and to be the faithful guardians of our homes." Clearly the Greeks had no moral qualms about consorting with prostitutes.

At the Olympics, which the Greeks invented, carnal pleasures were pursued with special vigor. Teams of exotic girls were shipped in from Asia Minor by enterprising *pornoboskoi* (literally "prostitute shepherds"). Beautiful and accomplished courtesans, these women seduced wealthy sports fans with their witty banter, while the humbler servants of Aphrodite plied their trade in *kineteria* (sex factories).

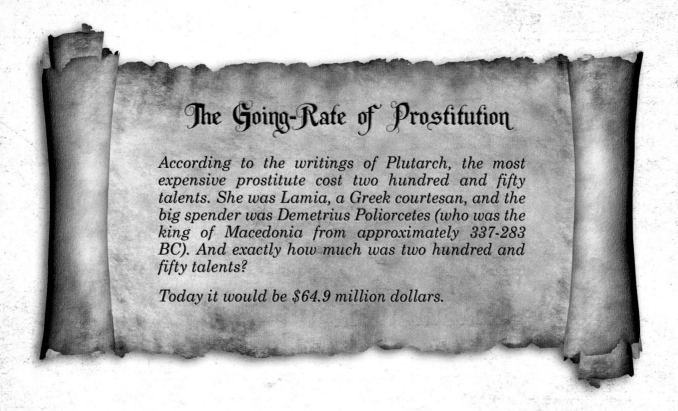

The Going-Rate of Prostitution

According to the writings of Plutarch, the most expensive prostitute cost two hundred and fifty talents. She was Lamia, a Greek courtesan, and the big spender was Demetrius Poliorcetes (who was the king of Macedonia from approximately 337-283 BC). And exactly how much was two hundred and fifty talents?

Today it would be $64.9 million dollars.

Not all Greek men, however, were enamored of prostitution, sacred or otherwise. The philosopher Diogenes thought the habit of paying for love ridiculous, once telling a crowd that he himself "met the goddess Aphrodite everywhere, and at no expense." When asked what he meant, Diogenes lifted up his tunic and pretended to masturbate.

Lesbian Ladies

The Greek island of Lesbos—where the term "lesbian" originated because communities of women gathered there to commune and share poetry—would seem to be an island full of women who desired sex with other women. In fact, the residents of Lesbos had quite an affinity for the opposite sex. This fondness was expressed with gusto. In ancient Athens, women from this island were known for their singular talent in performing sexual acts on men. In ancient times, a Greek woman was acting like a "lesbian" if she fellated all the men at a banquet.

ANCIENT GREEK POTTERY

CHAPTER FOUR

Ladies of Ancient Rome

*T*he ancient Romans loved sex. This is an undisputed fact, as a wealth of erotica from that era still survives today, showing in great detail the many and varied pleasures they delighted in. Enjoyment of sex was considered an essential part of life; better yet, they were free from any feelings of guilt or shame. Remember, this was BC, before Christ, long before any notions of shame were attached to sexual acts.

The Romans borrowed heavily from Greek culture. Aphrodite, the Greek goddess of love, became Venus to the Romans. Statues of her erotic union with Mars were displayed all over the empire. Though Romans appreciated both beauty and sex, they did not hold prostitutes in the same high esteem as the Greeks. They took a much more realistic, clear-eyed view of prostitution.

What the Romans did care about was class and social position. The highest class was senatorial, which included all men who served in the Senate and their families. This class was made up of noblemen of great wealth from ancient and elite families; serving in the Roman Senate was an unpaid position, and they were restricted from engaging in trade or business. A Senator had to be rich enough to devote all of his time to the higher calling of government service.

Rome had no middle class, and the gulf between the upper and lower classes ran deep and wide. In descending order, the lower classes included: *equestrians*—the tradesman class;

plebes—freeborn Roman citizens; *foreigners*—those who lived in other Roman territories; *libertines*—men or women who had once been slaves but had been officially set free by their masters; and *slaves*—the lowest of the low.

Roman slavery was not based upon race; slaves were frequently captured in battle or taken from conquered towns and brought to Rome. The slave trade was a booming business in Rome; the upper classes needed many slaves at their homes to support their lavish lifestyle. Any child born to a slave, no matter who fathered it, was automatically a slave. The easiest and most common object of desire for the elite Roman men were the household slaves. As the absolute property of their masters, they were there to gratify any sexual act. For a slave, sexually servicing their owner was not any more degrading than any other task they had to perform. It was simply a job.

The basic tenet of Roman sexuality was that one person dominated while the other submitted. At the top of the hierarchy was the elite Roman noble male; everything was geared to his pleasure. He was the dominator or the penetrator, if you will—the one who did things to others. The elite sought and bought all kinds of companionship, and the only reason a Roman man could be censured for extramarital sex was if it happened to involve the wife, son or daughter of another respectable noble.

So it was consciousness of their status rather than any prudish notions that governed sexual behavior among the Romans. An upper-class Roman matron, for example, prided herself on her virtue. She was expected to remain a virgin until marriage and once married, she did not have to engage in acts like fellatio. The noblemen of Rome turned to prostitutes for that sort of pleasure.

Prostitution was alive and well in ancient Rome. In fact, every April 27th the Romans celebrated the festival known as the Floralia. The ancient festival was originally celebrated to honor the goddess Flora, who represented flowers and fertility. However, prostitutes considered this day their own, as there was a legend,

Ladies of the Night

perhaps true, that a prostitute named Flora had bequeathed the huge fortune she'd earned in the trade to the common people to celebrate her birthday each year. The celebrations were wild and full of nudity, obscenity, and every conceivable kind of vulgarity.

FLORA, Louise Abbema, 1913

To this goddess, Flora, was dedicated Floralia—a festival in ancient Rome that celebrated fertility and drinking. The goddess Flora was also an icon for the prostitutes of ancient Rome.

Prior to the time of Caesar, there were no Roman laws on the books against prostitution; owning a brothel was a legitimate source of income. Any Roman, including slaves, was free to visit brothels. Their owners advertised with eye-catching signs outside their establishments. Buying and reselling slaves at auction was frequent activity of brothel owners, who wanted to maintain variety in their houses. The sex trade brought great profits to the owners of female slaves.

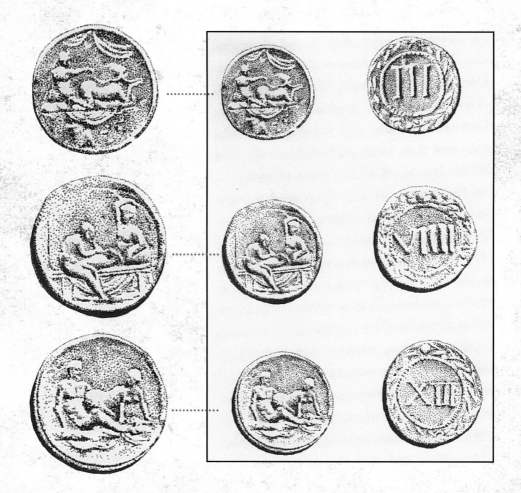

ENGRAVING OF "SPINTRIAE" purportedly found at Pompeii, 19th century

The *spintria* was a Roman token, found at Pompeii, that was assumed to have been used to pay prostitutes for their various services. And how do these brilliant archaeologists know this? Because the coins depict explicit sexual imagery (and actual acts). Not exactly rocket science to figure this one out!

Ladies of the Night

Like most everything else in Roman society, there were brothels for the noblemen and brothels for the lower classes. Most of the brothels were located in the Second District of the city, the busiest and most densely populated area of Rome. The regular brothels were generally filthy, smelling of gas from the lamps, poorly ventilated and decorated with obscene paintings and statuary.

The more refined establishments frequented by the upper classes were comfortable, beautifully decorated with fine art and kept slaves busy as hairdressers and makeup artists to attend to the Ladies, water boys to fill bidets, and waiters to fetch wine and food. The fanciest houses employed a secretary to assign names to Ladies, fix their price, and collect their fees. In all brothels a tablet was fixed outside each Lady's door, listing her name and price; she turned it over to say "Occupied" when she was engaged inside with a customer.

Brothels were stocked with slaves and "official" prostitutes—meaning they had officially registered with the city and been given a license. However, to officially register in this way meant that a woman was listed as a prostitute for life.

A Roman officer known as the *aedile* handled all official matters concerning prostitution. His government office was where Ladies registered and licenses were granted. The aedile also patrolled the district and entered brothels at various hours, checking to see that no business was conducted between daybreak and three in the afternoon. When fights broke out, he arrested and punished the offenders. He fined brothel-keepers if any of the women in their house were not registered. He insisted that prostitutes wear the correct garments prescribed by the law. It was also the aedile's job, when a prostitute filed a compliant, to sentence any customer of hers to pay the sum due to her. However, he was bound under law to enter a brothel only if he had the permission of his office, and only when accompanied by the proper authorities.

Another one of the aedile's duties was to drive out from the city any prostitutes who were unregistered; there were so many that this law was impossible to enforce consistently. Plenty of "illicit" prostitutes trolled the streets, circuses and famous Roman baths. Taverns were generally regarded as brothels, and waitresses offered favors for sale.

Unregistered prostitutes far outnumbered the "official count," and they too fell into a rigid hierarchy: French *Lorettes* were very charming, foreign, beautiful and expensive. *Doris* were famous for their enchanting figures and frequently disdained clothing, preferring to parade about in the nude. *Lupae* were "she-wolves" who trolled gardens and parks while actually howling to attract customers. *Noctilae* walked the streets at night; *Forariae* stood on country roads to attract travelers; *Bustuariae* hung around burial grounds and were often hired as mourners. *Copae* were servant girls at inns and taverns, and the *Gallinae* were thieves as well as prostitutes.

The three lowest-class and cheapest prostitutes were known as: *Blitidae*, named after a cheap drink served in the bars they frequented; the *Diobolares,* who were priced at two *obolis* (roughly equal to two cents); and the *Quadrantariae*, whose price was less than that of one American penny.

Oddly enough, Roman graveyards were a popular place for trysts with prostitutes. The great philosopher Seneca was particularly disturbed by this widespread practice, which he thought unhealthy and debauched. Still, the practice abounded, as couples fornicated among ancient Roman tombstones—many scrawled and carved with elaborate curses, heaping everlasting damnation on a lover who had scorned them in this life.

In addition to frequenting Ladies of the Night, rich Roman noblemen kept mistresses, of course. Some imported Greek and Syrian mistresses, as they were displeased with the service from rough native girls; these imported women were skilled in the arts of seduction.

Women known as *Delicatae* were well-kept women, usually from higher-class families. *Famosae* also came from well-off families, choosing to sell their bodies usually for extra money or

Ladies of the Night

to influence politics by means of using powerful men. They were not found working at brothels, inns, or taverns, nor were they seen walking about the shady spots of the city. Many invited clients to their own homes to be privately entertained.

The Delicatae and Famosae did not dress like prostitutes, and were distinguishable from virtuous Roman wives only by the superior elegance of their dress and the swarm of admirers that followed them around. These women enjoyed the patronage of rich and powerful men.

All in all, both the Greeks and the Romans created controlled, civilized systems for dealing with Ladies of the Night— far superior to the state of affairs in our present-day society.

WALL PAINTING OF A COUPLE, found in Pompeii

Man and wife or man and mistress, you be the judge....

CHAPTER FIVE
Ladies of Egypt

Ancient Egyptian culture, which flourished under a fiery sun amid swirling sands almost five thousand years ago, all began with the origin of the universe. The great sun-god Atum-Ra created the earth itself along with the first god and goddess through masturbation, as he had no one to mate with. From this act all the other deities and mankind itself were created.

The goddess Isis was venerated as the archetypical wife and mother. She married her brother, the god Osiris, who was murdered by his jealous brother. Osiris' body was then dismembered by his evil sibling and his body parts were scattered all over Egypt. His penis was thrown into the Nile, where it was swallowed by a fish. (Not quite Cain and Abel, is it?) Isis scoured the entire land and managed to recover all of the pieces of his body, then wrapped them up to form a whole body again. The devoted wife re-created a new penis for her husband and attached magic wings to her own body, which blew new life into her dead husband. The mummified Osiris is depicted in ancient art lying down with an erect penis, as Isis sweeps down upon him for one last act of intercourse and impregnation.

There was a strong link between Ladies and the divine in ancient Egypt. An Egyptian sacred prostitute (who was a highly regarded member of Egyptian society because of her association with different gods or goddesses, the complete opposite of a common streetwalker) advertised herself through her clothing and makeup. Some of these Ladies wore blue, beaded fish-net dresses. They painted their lips red, tattooed themselves on the breasts or thighs, and some went so far as to walk around in public totally nude. There is no evidence that these women were paid for these fertility-related acts, so the word "prostitute" as we think of it today is probably not an accurate description of such Ladies.

Some scholars believe that premarital sexual activity might have been a prerequisite for marriage. Far from being prostitutes, sexual activity on the part of young women was simply a "coming-of-age ritual" (literally!)—just as circumcision was one for males. With Egypt's heavy emphasis on fertility as the defining nature of a man or a woman, this idea is a highly likely probability.

Another theory is that young virgin girls joined itinerant performing groups—made up of dancers, singers and the like—and during their time with these groups they experienced their first sexual encounters. Sort of like touring with a rock band! If a girl became pregnant, she would then leave the troupe to head home to her family carrying the proof of her fertility. Motherhood was venerated, giving a woman a much higher status in society, so pregnancy was something to be proud of in ancient Egypt.

Our modern concepts regarding both sexuality and prostitution do not easily fit into this ancient society. Women operated under a totally different cultural imperative than women today, and we must view ancient Egyptian sexuality through different eyes. The female performers of this era—these so-called prostitutes—were treated with courtesy and respect, and there appeared to be a well-established link between these traveling performers and fertility, childbirth, religion and magic.

Ladies of the Night

Egyptians enjoyed sex for recreation as well as procreation. There was a delightful sense of adolescent freedom among Egyptians in terms of sexuality and a well-developed sense of romance as well, immortalized in their love poetry. Egyptian poetry of the time sings the praises of the beauty of a woman's body, with flowery odes to her thigh and breast and neck.

The culture was so steeped in sexuality that when the renowned Greek historian Herodotus visited Egypt he was shocked by the way that sex permeated the entire culture. According to medical lore of the time, a man losing his eyesight needed the urine of a virgin to cure his blindness. It was impossible, Herodotus complained, to find even one virgin in Egypt. There were very few prohibitions concerning sexual relations; there is literally no word in ancient Egyptian that can be translated as "virgin."

Despite the Egyptians' sexual openness, marriage was a very important institution; adultery attacked the fundamental basis of their society. They frowned upon adultery, or as they called it, "going to another house." In surviving texts, adulterous wives were thrown to the dogs or burnt alive. The man might also be executed, or only mutilated.

By far the most important aspect of Egyptian culture was having children. One of the hallmarks of Egyptian civilization was the notion of having heirs. No individual could be successful without heirs to carry-on his name and maintain his cult after death. The Egyptians invented the earliest versions of pregnancy tests and contraceptives, including an early version of the sponge and a contraceptive paste made of crocodile dung.

Much of what we know about Egyptian life was preserved on papyrus scrolls. These written records of Egyptian life represent only one to five percent of the population: the literate elite. Banquets were a popular form of relaxation, at least for the upper class. At such events food, alcoholic beverages, music, and dancing were common forms of entertainment.

A more earthy type of entertainment was offered by inns and beer houses of the time, where drinking often led to singing, dancing, and gaming, and men and women were free to interact with each other. Taverns stayed open late into the night, and patrons drank beer in such quantities that intoxication was not uncommon. In one ancient text, a teacher at a school of scribes chastens a student for his late-night activities: "I have heard that you abandoned writing and that you whirl around in pleasures, that you go from street to street and it reeks of beer. Beer makes him cease being a man. It causes your soul to wander.... Now you stumble and fall upon your belly, being anointed with dirt."

The national drink in ancient Egypt was beer, and all ancient Egyptians—rich and poor, male and female—drank great quantities of it. Wages were paid in grain, which was used to make two staples of the Egyptian diet: bread and beer.

The streets of larger towns had a number of "beer halls," and the same text quoted above also refers to the "harlots" who could be found there. Proverbs warning young men to avoid fraternization with "a woman who has no house" indicate that some form of prostitution did indeed exist in ancient Egyptian society. For instance, the "Instructions of Ankhsheshenqy" admonish, "He who makes love to a woman of the street will have his purse cut open on its side." During the Graeco-Roman period, brothels were known to exist near town harbors and could be identified by an erect phallus over the door, and tax records refer to houses that were leased for the purpose of prostitution.

Snefru, whom the Greeks called "the Good King," ruled over a land of calm and prosperity. He crowned himself the first living Sun God and, instead of the usual one monument, built a total of five pyramids for himself. Ancient papyri depict the king being rowed around a lake by young beauties wearing only fishnets for his amusement.

Ladies of the Night

His son and successor, the tyrannical Khufu (also known as Cheops) soon became known as "the bad King." He referred to himself as "Son of the Sun God" and according to legend, raised the immense sums of money needed to build his own pyramid by selling his own beautiful daughter into a brothel. This monument, paid for by his daughter's labors, became the famous pyramid of Giza, which was the tallest building ever constructed until the twentieth century and one of the seven ancient wonders of the world. The bad King's daughter decided that she would also build a pyramid for herself. Legend has it that every time she took a client, he had to bring her one stone, which went to building her own pyramid. This eventually became the second pyramid of Giza.

Certain private quarters of the royal household were devoted entirely to the women of the palace, including the queen, lesser wives, and concubines. It is from an ancient Egyptian word describing this situation that we have the word "harem."

FRAGMENTARY STATUE OF A WOMAN, POSSIBLY NEFERHETEPES,
ca. 4th Dynasty of Egypt

BUST OF CLEOPATRA

Cleopatra, while not a prostitute, is an example of one of the strongest, most independent (and most feared) women in Egyptian history. In keeping with her "independent" nature, Cleopatra bedded numerous men in her lifetime; including Caesar, Antony, and her brothers. She was not a shy Lady. Rather than submit to her Roman conquerors, Cleopatra induced a poisonous Egyptian cobra to bite her. Not exactly the simplest of suicides, but one that guaranteed her a spot in the history books!

CHAPTER SIX
Ladies of India

❧

Like the ancient Greeks, the ancient Indians took many of their cues from their gods and goddesses. In one of India's many creation myths, Heaven and Earth are the parents of all mankind. Heaven reached out to his daughter Earth, and with the passion created by the god of fire, spilled his seed onto Earth. From this seed came words and rituals. Arbitrators between the gods and humans also emerged from the seed; one of their functions was to distribute gifts from the gods to humans.

LAJJA GAURI, ca. 650 CE

The Lajja Gauri is an ancient Indian goddess representing abundance and fertility. She is also known as *uttanapad*, "she who crouches with legs spread."

Indian gods and goddesses had wives, lovers, pets, and children. They led very human lives, serving as models for mortal Indians to follow—sometimes literally. The god Krishna embodied passionate love and had quite a reputation as a ladies' man. Ancient Indian lore has it that a teenage girl was sneaking out of her house to meet the love god in the woods when her father caught her and forbade her from leaving. Heartbroken, she called out to him all night, "Krishna, Krishna!" Because she recited his holy name over and over, she was sent to the highest heaven to enjoy an eternity of bliss with him.

The *Rgveda,* a sacred collection of hymns within the Hindu Vedas, is one of the oldest surviving religious texts in any European language, having been composed more than 1000 years BC. *Rgveda* means praise, verse and knowledge in Sanskrit. Studying the *Rgveda* offers a glimpse into ancient Indian life, which alludes to a wide variety of seemingly modern conditions, including adultery, abortion, incest and prostitution.

The Hindu religion played a major part in the blatant sexuality of the early Indian people. Hinduism has a healthy, unrepressed outlook on human sexuality, and sexual pleasure is part of *kama,* one of the four goals of life. On matters such as birth control, sterilization, masturbation, homosexuality, bisexuality, petting and polygamy, Hindu scripture is tolerantly silent, neither calling them sins nor encouraging their practice. The two important exceptions to this understanding view of sex are adultery and abortion, both of which were considered to carry heavy karmic implications.

Still, adultery was apparently quite common in ancient India; male and female lovers of a married spouse were known as *jara* and *jatini.* In early days when currency was unknown and society functioned on a barter economy, gifts between lovers were equivalent to payment in cash. It is a difficult distinction to make: were the women willing partners showered with gifts by an adoring partner, or did they oblige their partners with sexual favors to receive gifts (i.e., cash)? Official prostitution as an actual profession appears in Indian literature a few centuries later, though it obviously existed in Indian society before then.

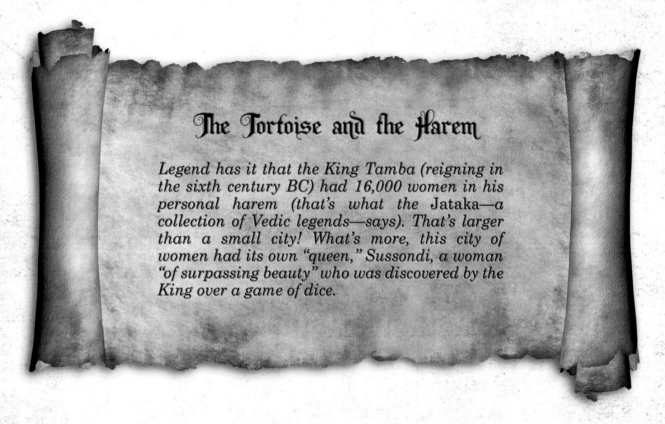

The Tortoise and the Harem

Legend has it that the King Tamba (reigning in the sixth century BC) had 16,000 women in his personal harem (that's what the Jataka—a collection of Vedic legends—says). That's larger than a small city! What's more, this city of women had its own "queen," Sussondi, a woman "of surpassing beauty" who was discovered by the King over a game of dice.

As always, there were different classes of prostitutes, even in ancient India. The lowest class doubled as housemaids to their master. Next was the middle-class prostitute, who demanded pay for her favors and was often artistically inclined, offering dance and music along with her sexual services. In these Ladies' cases, the husband usually lived off of his wife's income and acted as her pimp. The highest-level Ladies were known as *Ganikas*, and their job was officially recognized by the state. To reach this rarified position, the Lady had to be well-versed in the famous "64 Arts." A Ganika was beautiful, intelligent, and talented in many ways, worthy of royal treatment everywhere she went.

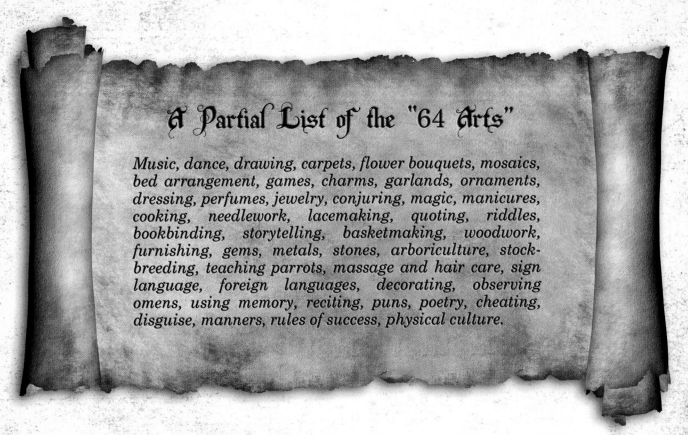

A Partial List of the "64 Arts"

Music, dance, drawing, carpets, flower bouquets, mosaics, bed arrangement, games, charms, garlands, ornaments, dressing, perfumes, jewelry, conjuring, magic, manicures, cooking, needlework, lacemaking, quoting, riddles, bookbinding, storytelling, basketmaking, woodwork, furnishing, gems, metals, stones, arboriculture, stock-breeding, teaching parrots, massage and hair care, sign language, foreign languages, decorating, observing omens, using memory, reciting, puns, poetry, cheating, disguise, manners, rules of success, physical culture.

Ambapali was the most famous courtesan in India some 500 years BC. She was discovered as an infant under a mango tree in the royal gardens of the ancient Indian capital city of Vaishali. She grew up to be a lady of incomparable beauty and charm. Her suitors were so numerous that she was given the official title of state royal courtesan (Ganika) of Vaishali to avoid fights between them. Her presence did much to enhance the prestige of the city.

Stories of her legendary charms spread to the neighboring hostile kingdom of Mahadha. Their King, Bimbasara, became so bewitched by her legend that he invaded Vaishali simply to woo her. He successfully romanced her, and she bore him a son. But Ambapali's legend lives because of her association with Buddha.

As bright as she was beautiful, Ambapali was continually searching for truth and wisdom. When Buddha visited her city and camped with his followers in her grove, she went out to hear him speak. Buddha was said to be very taken with her. "This

Ladies of the Night

woman moves in worldly circles and is a favorite of kings and princes; yet her heart is calm and composed. Young in years, rich, surrounded by pleasures, she is thoughtful and steadfast. This, indeed, is rare in the world. Women, as a rule, are scant in wisdom and deeply immersed in vanity; but she, although living in luxury, has acquired the wisdom of a master, taking delight in piety, and able to receive the truth in its completeness," said Buddha.

Ambapali invited Buddha and his disciples to dine with her; he accepted with a silent nod. On her way home, Ambapali excitedly told her neighbors, a wealthy family named Licchavi which was of princely rank, of the forthcoming visit by her honored guest. "Give up this meal to us for one hundred thousand!" implored her neighbors. Ambapali refused, saying she would not give up such an honor for the riches of the entire city.

The Licchavi then traveled to the groves themselves, where Buddha was dazzled by their fine carriages and magnificent dress. At the conclusion of their talk, the Licchavi invited Buddha to dine with them the following day. "I have promised to dine tomorrow with Ambapali, the courtesan," Buddha replied. Her neighbors bowed and departed politely, but threw up their hands as soon as they were out of sight. "A worldly woman has outdone us; we have been left behind by a frivolous girl!"

Ambapali did have the honor of serving Buddha and his followers the next day; she fed them sweet rice and cakes and at the conclusion of the meal humbly offered her mansion and lands to him. He accepted, and Ambapali thereafter renounced the life of a courtesan to become one of his disciples, eventually attaining the rank of *arhat*, one who has become totally enlightened and realized the goal of nirvana. (P.S. Her son became a monk as well.)

King Akbar (the Philosopher King) is widely considered the greatest ruler in Indian history. He was a great leader, warrior, hunter, a lover of nature and the arts, expert sportsman and philosopher. During his reign from 1556 to 1606, India expanded into a huge empire, which he ruled efficiently by means of military governors in each region and ingenious bureaucracy. And Akbar was quite a ladies' man.

The King acquired an almost incalculable number of mistresses and marital partners through a steady stream of marriage alliances with neighboring royalty, all for the purposes of expanding his empire. The population of his harem soon grew immense: around 5,000 maidens, many of whom were older women, although there were also young servant girls and Amazons from Russia who served as armed guards. Though Akbar was a devout Muslim and the Koran limits the number of wives a man can have to four, Akbar possessed over 300 wives. Ironically, he later decreed that "it was best for ordinary men to have only one wife!"

During this era, King Akbar dealt with Ladies efficiently. A superintendent and a clerk were appointed to register the names of those citizens who went to prostitutes or wanted to take some of them to their houses. Such relationships were acceptable, provided the toll collectors permitted it. "His Majesty established a wine shop near the palace.... The prostitutes of the realm collected at the shop could scarcely be counted, so large was their number.... The dancing girls used to be taken home by the courtiers. If any well-known courtier wanted to have a virgin, they should first have His Majesty's permission," noted an observer of the time.

The Kama Sutra

No discussion of the Ladies of India would be complete without mentioning the most famous sexual book of all time. The Kama Sutra made its debut sometime in the third century. Several authors contributed short works on various aspects of eroticism; a section on courtesans was written with the aid of a famous Lady from the ancient city of Pataliputra. The texts were collected into one volume by the Indian philosopher and sage Vatsyayana. Originally intended for the elite, aristocratic men of Indian society, this guide has proven an invaluable aid to millions of people all over the world.

The Kama Sutra provides an extensive classification of all things sexual. Sections include various sexual positions, advice on acquiring and satisfying a wife, the arts of courtesans, and how to attract others. Bites, scratches, moaning, the four types of love, the eight stages of oral intercourse; the Kama Sutra covers all this and much more in great detail.

The Kama Sutra also helpfully provides solutions for every conceivable sexual predicament, including an ancient method for penis enlargement (it involved hanging weights from the penis). The Kama Sutra addresses the sexual needs of women, encouraging men to be skillful and considerate sex partners and tutoring them on how best to set the mood. This has made the Kama Sutra extremely popular with all the Ladies of the world: past, present and future.

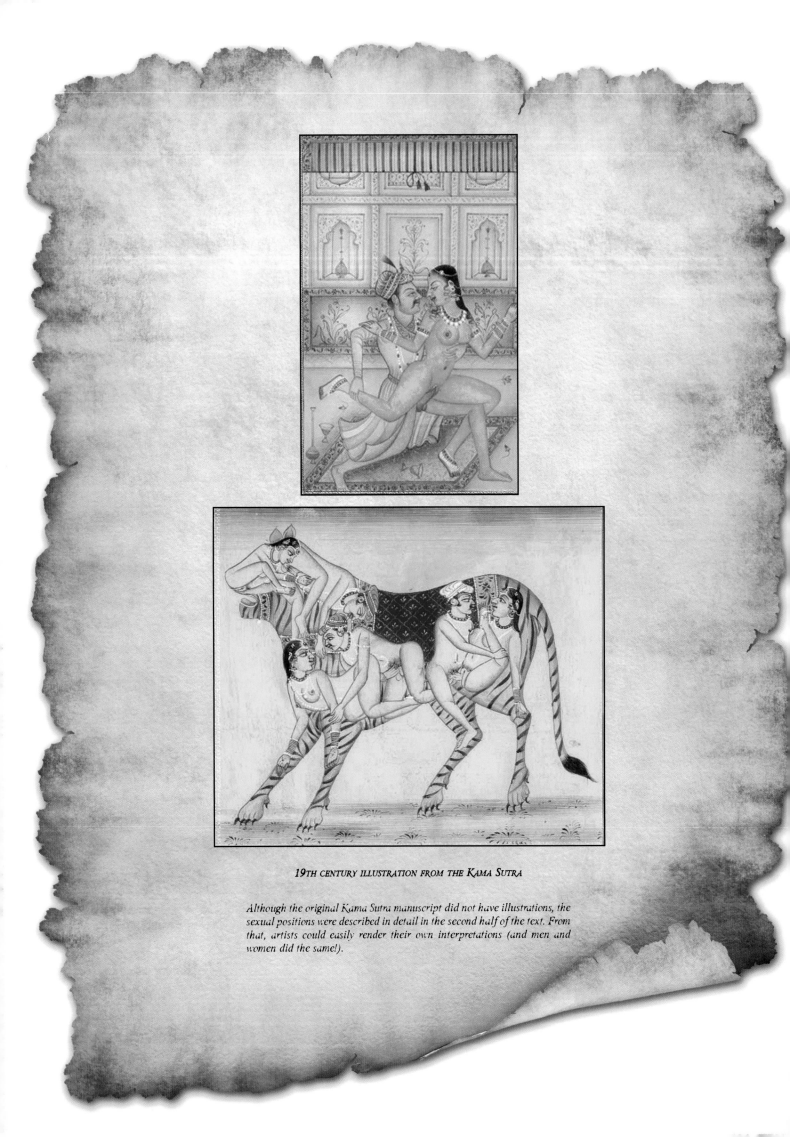

19TH CENTURY ILLUSTRATION FROM THE *KAMA SUTRA*

Although the original Kama Sutra manuscript did not have illustrations, the sexual positions were described in detail in the second half of the text. From that, artists could easily render their own interpretations (and men and women did the same!).

CHAPTER SEVEN

Ladies of China

The Chinese prized balance and equilibrium in all areas of their lives: diet, exercise, love and sex. The Chinese expression for sexual intercourse, "clouds and rain," dates back to their earliest history. This metaphor described the heavens making love to the earth and represented perfect order in the universe.

Ancient Chinese philosophies about sex were greatly influenced by three schools of thought: Confucionism, Taoism, and Buddhism. The first two were very similar in their attitudes toward sex: the ultimate goal of Confucionism was the continuation of the family line. Taoism was about promoting life. Followers of Buddha sought to transcend sexuality, life and even death in order to attain enlightenment.

Sex played a huge role in each of these schools of thought. At the heart of both Confucianism and Taoism lay the concept of yin and yang: opposite forces that made up the universe, nature and the human body. Ancient Chinese physicians believed that yin and yang were present in both men and women in the form of essences. A man's essence was expressed through his semen. A woman's essence was expressed through the vital energy she expended during sex and climax. It was the man's duty to control a woman's responses in order to take on her essence, and he tried not to climax.

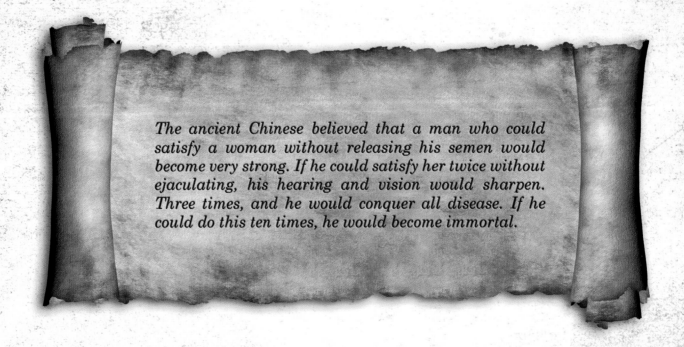

The ancient Chinese believed that a man who could satisfy a woman without releasing his semen would become very strong. If he could satisfy her twice without ejaculating, his hearing and vision would sharpen. Three times, and he would conquer all disease. If he could do this ten times, he would become immortal.

In their quest for immortality, Chinese men read ancient Dao sex manuals, which were runaway bestsellers fully three hundred years BC! They were explicitly detailed how-to manuals that provided men with a blueprint for satisfying women while preserving their precious male yang. A Taoist man usually chose a teenage girl as a sex partner, as she had not yet been contaminated by childbirth. Their essence was considered especially potent.

However, young girls were not skilled in the arts of love and the complicated sexual positions in the sex manuals. To learn, they read "pillow books," sex manuals to help young lovers which were written in flowery language, using such terms as "the jade stalk," "the red flower and its heady perfume," and "the golden lotus."

Ladies of the Night

PRINT FROM A "PILLOW BOOK," *Kitagawa Utamaro, 1788*

This picture shows an actor/prostitute wooing a client; sealing the deal, in other words. Pillow books were like the Japanese Kama Sutra that gave geishas and prostitutes in Japan references as to certain sexual positions and methods. Pillow Books used poetic, flowery language which was much less blatant than that of its Indian sister book.

Confucius, legendary Chinese philosopher, lived and taught in the fifth century BC. Three centuries later, his teachings, known as the way of humanity, became a popular national philosophy and in the second century BC, Confucionism became the official religion of China. Unlike Dao, which stressed the longevity of the man, Confucionism placed the utmost importance on family and procreation. This school of thought completely changed China's social structure and ideas of sexual duty and pleasure.

Confucian teachings were all about extending the family as a social institution, not increasing individual pleasure. The ideal Chinese woman was no longer a nubile teenager; giving birth was now seen as a plus instead of a minus. Sex manuals of the time reflect the change; they were no longer geared solely toward the man's pleasure. They stressed the optimum positions for impregnation, and the best positions for creating male children. Confucius also mentions female pleasure. Physicians at the time realized that if women enjoyed sex, they would want to have more of it, thereby increasing the size of the family. Manuals of the day made sex seem as enticing as possible to women as a means of begetting more children.

China was an agrarian society with a high infant-mortality rate. Large families were necessary to harvest crops and run farms. One of the surest ways to guarantee a large family was the practice of polygamy. Though uncommon, a wealthy Chinese man might have several wives. The first was the official, legal wife. The subsequent wives were considered concubines.

One emperor in ancient China presided over 121 wives, consorts and concubines. In the course of the year, he was supposed to service each and every one of them. Assisting him were his sex secretaries, who kept careful records of each encounter and each woman's special needs. Men of this era used potent aphrodisiacs to bolster their performance.

Marriage in ancient China was a business deal; Buddhism openly sanctioned sex outside the marriage. Men sought out sexual relief with no threat to the family unit.

Brothels were actually an escape for Chinese men from the demands of sex! Upper-class businessmen would work out of these establishments, which brings to mind the dealmaking that occured in Roman bathhouses. Here they escaped their families and wives, cut deals, did business and relaxed in the company of other men and courtesans, whose main job requirement was to soothe overstressed men.

Upscale brothels were about socializing and relaxing; low-end establishments offered only sex with older, cheaper and less attractive prostitutes. Some of these lower-class brothels contained bamboo lamps with red silk covers—the very first red-light district.

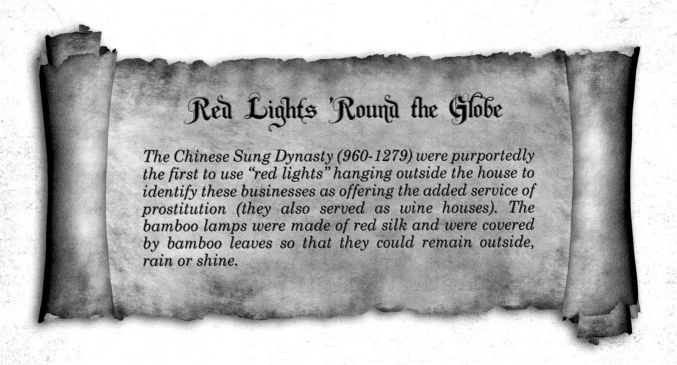

Red Lights 'Round the Globe

The Chinese Sung Dynasty (960-1279) were purportedly the first to use "red lights" hanging outside the house to identify these businesses as offering the added service of prostitution (they also served as wine houses). The bamboo lamps were made of red silk and were covered by bamboo leaves so that they could remain outside, rain or shine.

References to prostitution in the ancient histories are spotty, but it is possible to speculate about the development of government-owned brothels. Some researchers believe that China's first brothels were established in the seventh century BC by the famous statesman and philosopher Guan Zhong, who used them as a means of increasing the state's income. Guan, who was the premier of the State of Chi in the period of Duke Huan, established seven government-owned markets with housing for 700 women in Duke Huan's palace. Whether they were public brothels or merely evidence of his sexual extravagance is open to debate.

The King of Yue established a widow's camp on a mountain to supply sexual outlets for his armies during the Warring States period. Then the famous Emperor Wu recruited female camp followers for his armies; these women were called *ying-chi* (camp harlots).

However the custom started, it is clear that the institution of government-run prostitution reached its peak in the Tang and Sung dynasties. In the Tang dynasty, some prostitutes were connected with local governments, and their lives and business activities were almost totally controlled by local officials. Another class of prostitutes was controlled by the imperial government; these women lived in Pingkangli, a special district of Changan (the capital), and had greater freedom to conduct their own businesses. Private commercial prostitution became most highly developed during the Ming and Ching dynasties. In this later era, the cities of Suzhou, Hangzhou, Nanjing, Yangzhou, Shanghai, Beijing, Tianjin, and Kuangzhou were all famous for their flourishing prostitution trade.

In ancient China, where women led very proscribed lives, they would sometimes become courtesans, who entertained men for a living and served as both their friend and lover. When a man would travel, he would also take along the courtesan. Courtesans with literary, musical, or dancing ability were especially desirable companions, and many became famous historical figures.

One example was Chao Fei-yan (Flying Swallow Chao), courtesan to Emperor Han Cheng Ti. During their lovemaking, Fei-yan enchanted the emperor with her sexual technique; she made him feel that intercourse was effortless, yet utterly satisfying. Before they made love, according to one biography of the courtesan, the Emperor just gazed at her beauty for the first several hours.... Eventually he demoted the original queen and

Ladies of the Night

put Fei-yan in her place. Fei-yan is famous in Chinese history because she was essentially a prostitute who became queen of her own empire in China.

Another famous courtesan was Li Shih-shih, prostitute during the reign of emperor Huei Tsung. Those men lucky enough to sleep with her sang her praises in the most flowery language; she was described as "delicate as an orchid and graceful as a peony." The emperor became so enamored of Shih-shih that he disregarded the advice of several ministers and the jealousy of his queen and concubines to make love with her at every opportunity. When one of his concubines jealously asked him what was so special about Shih-shih, the emperor replied, "None of you knows about the art of love. With her, I never have to labor, and yet she offers me so much pleasure. In bed, she is always so lively and so full of fun. Compared with her, all of you are like beauties made of clay or wood."

Su Xiaoxiao was another of the most famous courtesans in Chinese history; sadly, her story ends after only nineteen years (circa 501), when she died of a terminal disease. Her legend—of being a poet and great beauty among other talents—lives on today in China, with a tomb dedicated to the ancient Lady.

TOMB OF SU XIAOXIAO

Chinese wives and concubines were expected to remain at home. Though it wasn't unheard of for a woman to take a lover, adultery was a disruption to the all-important family unit and was punishable by death. Women paid dearly for the sin of adultery, not that it was easy for them to get around, as they practiced the ancient ritual of foot-binding. The Chinese believed that small feet on a woman were sensual; the ritual began with a palace dancer who wrapped her feet in brightly colored silk when she danced for the palace court. Tiny feet wrapped in silk ribbons became a sexual turn-on. Men were never allowed to see the bare feet of their wives; they were considered a highly erotic object.

Prostitution, whether institutionalized or private, became completely ingrained in the Chinese culture. By the thirteenth century, Marco Polo reported that there were an estimated 20,000 women in China engaged in prostitution. Meanwhile, China's neighbor to the east, Japan, was establishing its own culture of exotic lovemaking and beautiful Ladies.

PORTRAIT OF MARCO POLO, 16th century

Marco Polo discussed the status of Asian prostitution in his travel writings:

And again I tell you another thing... that inside the town dare live no sinful woman...but...they all live outside in the suburbs. And you may know that there is so great a multitude of them for the foreigners that no man could believe it, for I dare tell you in truth that they are quite twenty thousand who all serve men for money, and they all find a living....

CHAPTER EIGHT
Ladies of Japan

Japan's sex and prostitution practices were largely influenced by religions of the time, similar to the neighboring Chinese culture. According to legend, the sexual congress of heaven and earth produced the first Japanese gods, among them Izanagi and Izanami, "the male who invites" and "the female who invites." After the earth was made, the two gods descended upon it and became husband and wife, shyly discovering each other's body parts: "I wish to unite this source-place of my body to the source-place of thy body." The islands they created resulted in a series of gods and goddesses, and Japanese society was born.

The Japanese had their own unique beliefs about sex; there was no concept of original sin. The Japanese believed that the family was the backbone of society; so long as men provided for their families and fathered children, they were free to cavort with prostitutes and concubines.

Unlike their Chinese counterparts, Japanese Ladies of the seventh century took multiple husbands and lovers. Aside from a man's wife, the prostitute played a vital role in Japanese society as a stress reliever.

COURTESAN PAINTING A SCREEN, *woodcut, 18th century*

The man in the background is watching his robed courtesan paint a screen. Most likely he's taking a break from…ahem….

Prostitutes were portrayed flatteringly and referred to as Buddhist goddesses of mercy, as they were performing a merciful service for men. Sexual urges needed to be relieved; prostitutes were necessary and valued.

Japanese prostitution begins with a legend about the *asobi* (derived from a word meaning "to play") who were professional

Ladies of the Night

musical and sexual entertainers and were actually spiritual descendents of the Dread Female of Heaven. According to the legend, eight asobi were dispatched to various parts of the region by the Emperor Koko in the ninth century.

No. 9 Girls, hand-colored photo, possibly by Kusakabe Kimbei

This hand-colored silver print is a group portrait of prostitutes in the Shimpuro Brothel in Yokohama. Based on these girls' kimonos, they were most likely asobi, which were the classiest of the Japanese Ladies.

Oe Yikitoki wrote in the late tenth century: "The younger women melt men's hearts with rouge and powder and songs and smiles.... If there are husbands, they censure their wives because their lovers are too few. If there are parents, they wish only that their daughters were fortunate enough to be summoned by many customers. This has become the custom, although no human feeling is involved."

Later, the eleventh-century courtier Fujiwara Akihira described the asobi as being quite accomplished. He wrote: "Her vigor in soliciting lovers, her knowledge of all the sexual positions, the merits of her lute strings and buds of wheat [flowery words for female genitalia], and her mastery of the dragon's flutter and tiger's treat techniques—all are her endowments...."

The business of prostitution was regulated by Japanese authorities beginning in the thirteenth century; it is most renowned for the period of the sixteenth century. It was then that Japanese government officials set aside licensed quarters with official registered prostitutes. The legal sex industry in most cities was limited to controlled districts, referred to in English as the "pleasure quarters." In premodern times these districts were quite literally gated communities. All prostitutes, called *yujo*, were required to live and work within their confines. In large cities, at least, a private, illegal sex industry also existed, but private prostitutes and their support staff of pimps and keepers faced frequent and often rather arbitrary legal sanctions. Sometimes the women who worked in the private sex industry were forced to serve in the pleasure quarters for extended periods without pay.

Yujo is a category that included a long list of specific titles for women, depending upon rank. The highest-ranking were called *tayu*. These women had great authority within the pleasure quarters and considerable autonomy. Despite their status, however, they remained legally bound to a brothel.

In the sixteenth century, the yujo's fabled counterpart arose and left an indelible image on the public's mind: the *geisha*. The very first geishas were reportedly the beautiful and talented daughters of aristocrats; contrary to modern-day beliefs, a geisha was not always a prostitute. Geisha meant "artist," and these women were highly trained in singing, dancing and performing tea ceremonies. Only occasionally did they have intimate relationships with their most valued clients.

However, the history of the geisha reaches back to the earliest kabuki performers of the late sixteenth and early seventeenth centuries, and at one point geishas included both men and women who not only performed on stage but also freely sold sexual favors.

Geisha women WERE prostitutes at one time!

They were allowed into the government-controlled brothel district under agreements that kept them from competing for customers with the house professionals. The role of the geisha was to provide an artistic interlude in an evening's entertainment that otherwise inclined toward more carnal activities...i.e., sex! While the geisha typically had true artistic talents, she was used for sex as well.

During the nineteenth century geishas grew rapidly in popularity and stature until they became more highly regarded by the male clientele than the previously prestigious ranks of yujo from the district itself.

Following the founding of a new government in 1868, overhauls of the country's legal system changed the conduct of legal prostitution. In 1872 the government liberated all prostitutes and geishas from their debts and allowed them to return to their homes. Many chose to do just that, but a significant number preferred to stay in the sex industry, which remained under the control of the individual prefectures rather than the state until 1900.

Eventually, due to reasons of public health, geishas and prostitutes were required to obtain separate licenses (some Ladies had both). By the end of the nineteenth century, geisha women were not required to have sex with their male patrons unless there was some sort of contractual agreement...just like marriage!

Much of what has scandalized Western observers of Japanese sexuality through the ages boils down to a simple but crucial cultural difference: the Christian West traditionally idealized virginity and purity; Japan idealized sex.

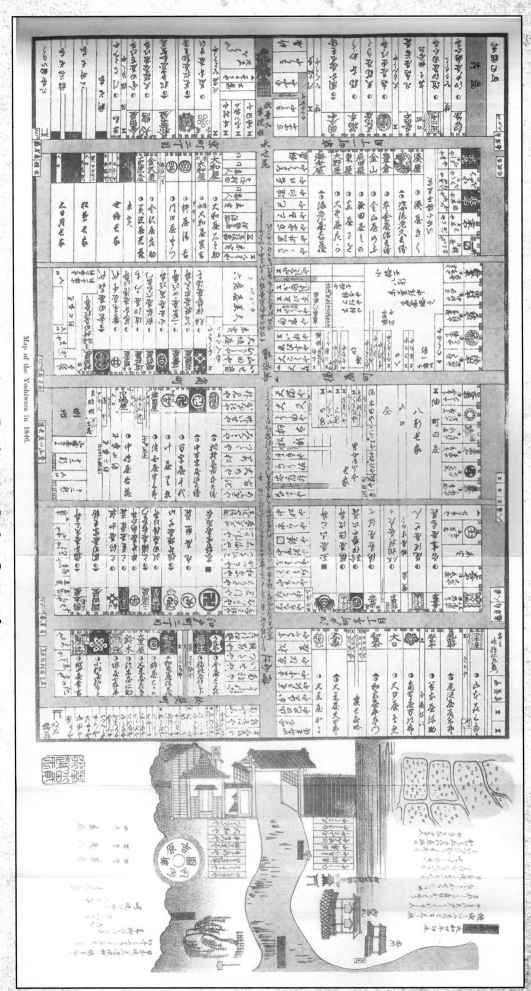

Map of the Yoshiwara in 1846.

THE 19TH CENTURY RED LIGHT DISTRICT IN JAPAN

CHAPTER NINE

Ladies of the Bible

*A*prostitute is one of the stars of the New Testament! And please, don't just take my word for it—study the subject yourself, or ask your preacher or rabbi.

MARY MAGDALENE IN THE CAVE, *Jules Joseph Lefebvre, 1876*

Prostitute or not prostitute? That is the question. Artists typically depicted Mary as having long hair which covers her shoulders—maybe covering up her adultery? Either way, my gospel says: Mary was a Lady, tried and true.

Before we talk further about Mary Magdalene and Jesus Christ, let's clarify a few points, since my assumption is almost all of you reading this have very little in the way of facts when it comes to these very important New Testament figures. They both did indeed exist, historical records show us.

But it's important to note that the historical person in Christianity referred to as the Son of God is actually incorrectly called Jesus Christ by his followers. Jesus Christ was not his name, and has never been his name! His birth name and title (we know from the Roman records kept by Josephus, the Hebrew scribe who kept track of such matters) was Rabbi Y'sua Ben Yosef—or, Rabbi Jesus, Son of Joseph.

For those of you, and I suspect it's almost all of you, who have never heard him called that, it's both historically and literally ACCURATE. He was indeed a Jewish Rabbi, and his last name was never Christ, nor did any of his followers, we would assume, ever call him Christ. They would correctly call him, in the Jewish community he lived in, "Rabbi" (Teacher). Since he had a title, he would probably not have been called simply Jesus (in Hebrew, that's Y'sua, not to be confused with another Hebrew name, Yoshua/Joshua). That would have been rude.

"Christ" comes from the Latin word *Cristo* meaning Messiah (from the Hebrew word "Messiach" or "deliverer") or King ("Melech"). That title is still used today, as in The Christ Child, or The Christ. "Christ" is a title, not a name—never has been.

There are people who swear that Jesus' parents were named Mr. and Mrs. Christ. Now you know differently. Again, if you don't believe me, ask your minister, pastor or priest.

Now that we have that out of the way, we all know the story about Mary Magdalene, the prostitute. The New Testament tells us she was about to be stoned to death by a mob for adultery in accordance with the Jewish laws of the time when all of a sudden the Rabbi steps forward and says to the crowd, "Who among you is without sin? Let those without sin cast the first stone." Or words to that effect.

It should be noted that no one who wrote any of the Gospels was an eyewitness to any of the events they wrote about, nor were the Gospels written until many years after the events they described took place. Furthermore, at the Council of Nicea, the Emperor Caesar Constantine (the first Roman Caesar to convert to Christianity in 312 AD) and his council outlawed many other Gospels containing stories of Mary Magdalene, and declared that Matthew, Mark, Luke and John were the only officially accepted Gospels.

Whether or not the event with the angry mob actually happened, and whether the woman in question was really Mary Magdalene is not the issue. Let's take a look at what is really going on. And kindly forgive me for stirring the pot a bit. It's a subject worth discussing.

Here is a Rabbi who makes a bold public statement. In essence, he says, "Don't kill this prostitute [or presumed prostitute] just because she does what she does." Yes, she may have sinned, he implies, but maybe that's none of your business. Maybe that's God's business (I would assume the Rabbi is referring to his Father, not to himself. In these areas, I admit I get lost. I am never clear when God is mentioned whether that means only the Father, or if it means only the Son, or if it means the Father and Son and Holy Ghost, collectively referred to as the Holy Trinity).

So here we have the Messiah, the Son of God and/or God himself saying, "Don't kill or harm prostitutes." Interesting.

The New Testament goes on to tell us how this one-time prostitute becomes his most favored companion—and even, perhaps, his wife! Yes. You read correctly. There is a very real dialogue currently going on in the Christian theological world about this very topic. I didn't invent this.

Incidentally, the reason there is such heated discussion regarding the issue of "was a prostitute the wife of the Rabbi or not?" comes from the custom and tradition of the Jewish people of the time. You may have heard the phrase "Behind every great man walks a great woman." That phrase refers to Mary Magdalene and the Rabbi. One would assume that He was comfortable with the idea that a prostitute was walking right behind him.

However, The Old Testament (or "The Bible") tells us that only the wife of a man is allowed to walk behind him. They are both making a very public statement: "She is my wife. I am her husband."

And again, whether the prostitute became the Rabbi's wife, was his favorite, or just followed behind him wherever he went doesn't really concern me. What I want to focus on is what the Rabbi apparently thinks about adultery, prostitutes and prostitution.

And here is my thought:

Isn't the Rabbi really saying prostitutes are not to be punished by human beings? Isn't the Rabbi saying if she sinned, haven't you all sinned? Isn't the Rabbi saying leave her alone?

This is a very emotional issue for people of the Christian faith, so I won't dwell too long here. I will leave you with the following. The two most important women in all of Christianity are: Mary, the Mother of God (or the Rabbi's Mother), and Mary Magdalene...a prostitute.

Ladies of the Night

THE LAST SUPPER, *Leonardo Da Vinci, 1495-98*

This famous Da Vinci painting appears to show Mary Magdalene seated at Jesus' right-hand side. The "V" design between them, some scholars insist, is a sign that Mary Magdalene was either his close confidant, his "favorite," or his wife. We shouldn't forget, however, that Da Vinci lived many hundreds of years after Christ died, and in any case, this is simply a work of art. Still, the prostitute Mary Magdalene's prominence in the New Testament is certainly food for thought.

Mary Magdalene may have been one of the two most important women in the New Testament, but there are other stories about so-called "wicked women."

To this day the name Jezebel brings up the image of a wanton hussy—perhaps because in the Old Testament she is referred to as painting her eyes, fixing her hair and putting on makeup before facing her imminent death. Strangely enough, given how her name has come to mean "ultimate harlot," she was never a prostitute, though she did worship Baal gods, whose pagan religious ceremonies included ritual prostitution.

It is therefore religious differences more than any sexual act that account for Jezebel's reputation as the most evil woman in the Old Testament: her refusal to worship God. As Queen of Israel, wife of King Ahab, Jezebel was a woman comfortable with seizing power. Her raging ambition led her to lie, cheat, murder prophets of the Lord (who foresaw her grisly death) and, in the bloodiest and most brutal episodes of the Old Testament, be thrown out a window to her death and eaten by dogs.

Now, was Jezebel painted "bad" merely because she empowered herself and acted like a man? Had she been male, she would have been seen as ambitious. Because she's a woman who wears makeup she's a slut. A double standard, even then...and maybe that's what this book is all about. Women should be allowed to act more like men, if you will: that is, decide for themselves what their ethics and sexual choices will be, and act upon them!

Delilah, the other "bad" girl of the Old Testament, fared a bit better. Though not officially a prostitute, she is infamous for betraying her lover Samson, the strongest man in the world. Samson, one of the Judges of Israel, governed the Hebrew people and slayed thousands of Philistines, his sworn enemy. He was strong enough to kill a lion with his bare hands and a hundred Philistines all by himself. But even the world's toughest man could be weakened by a woman's wiles. One might wonder...if Delilah had wanted to charge for her "wares," what might Samson have paid? What do you think? In any case, the Philistines bribed Delilah with silver to discover the source of her lover's amazing power.

SAMSON AND DELILAH, *Francesco Morone, 16th century*

The story of Samson and Delilah, depicted in this painting by Francesco Morone, has horrified men for centuries. In the Old Testament, Samson falls in love with Delilah and tells her his secret: that the power of his strength comes from his uncut hair. One day, while Samson is asleep on her lap, she has a servant cut off his hair, allowing him to be captured and imprisoned.

Three times she attempted to learn Samson's secret; three times he tricked her and escaped capture. Finally, just before falling asleep in her lap, Delilah said, in so many words, "If you really loved me you would tell me!" The infatuated Samson revealed that he possessed superhuman strength because he had never cut his hair as part of his faithful service to God. Delilah had a servant cut his locks while he slept. God—and his strength—deserted Samson, who was finally captured by the Philistines, blinded, tormented and chained like an animal.

After her act of treachery, the Old Testament makes no further mention of Delilah, although Samson, whose power returned as his hair grew in prison, eventually pulled down an entire building with his chains, killing 3,000 Philistines at once. But Delilah's name and story will forever be associated with foolish men, temptress women, the power of sex and the betrayal of love for money.

RAHAB OF JERICHO
from Hans (Jan) Collaert, Antwerp, 1566-1628

According to the Old Testament, a prostitute named Rahab assisted Israelite spies in Jericho. The spies, in return for the information, promised to save her and her family during the planned military invasion as long as she fulfilled her part of the deal by keeping the details of the contact with them secret and leaving a sign on her house that would be a marker for the soldiers to avoid her residence. She keeps her word and her family is spared. Eventually, Rahab left prostitution, joined the Jewish people and became an honorable married woman.

CHAPTER TEN
Roman Emperors...

and Their Wives

---

eanwhile in Rome, the Emperor Claudius was installed by the Imperial Guard after the murder of the notoriously evil Caligula in 41 AD—mainly because they still needed a job after killing off their old boss. The new Emperor limped, had a stutter, and was considered by his family to be an idiot. Ironically, he had survived his relatives Tiberius and Caligula's reigns of terror because of his disabilities and non-threatening appearance. Claudius attained his position basically because he was the last living adult male in his family line. Surprisingly, given his reputation, he actually proved to be an effective leader and took a particular interest in Roman expansion, including the conquering of Britain.

However, his wife Messalina was the more interesting half of the new royal couple. Messalina was the emperor's first cousin and had been closely aligned with Caligula's depraved inner circle. The kindest possible way to describe her would be "nymphomaniac."

Claudius himself traveled to Britain with his troops in 43 AD, at which point the city was left to Messalina, and she turned the city into her private boudoir. Roman sources claim that Messalina used sex to enforce her power and control politicians, that she owned a brothel under an assumed name, organized orgies for upper-class women, and sold her influence to Roman nobles and foreign notables.

With a veil draped over her head, the Empress used to sneak out at night to visit taverns and dark alleys, searching for men. On one such excursion, drunk on wine, she shamelessly danced naked on a wooden platform in the Forum. Messalina redecorated a bedroom of the palace to resemble a brothel, hung the name of Rome's most renowned prostitute on the door, then disrobed, gilded the nipples of her breasts, and invited the male public to enter and be entertained at no more than the legally regulated fee. She proved quite popular.

Emboldened by the heavy traffic, she challenged a particularly notorious Roman prostitute named Scylla to an all-night sex competition—betting that she could entertain more men than her famous rival. Scylla gave up at dawn when each woman had taken twenty-five lovers, but Messalina saw no reason to stop copulating until well into the morning. She was said to be exhausted but not yet satisfied.

The famous Roman poet and satirist Juvenal wrote of Messalina's contest:

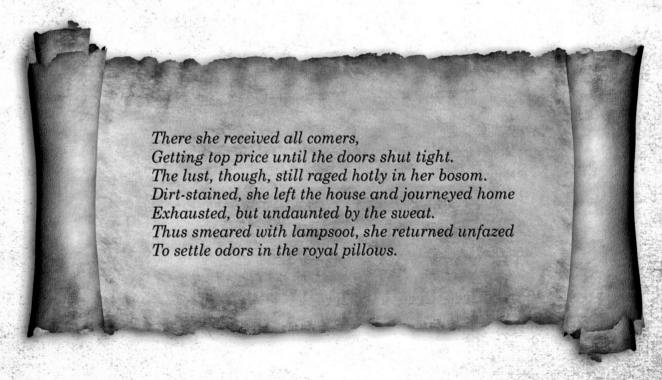

There she received all comers,
Getting top price until the doors shut tight.
The lust, though, still raged hotly in her bosom.
Dirt-stained, she left the house and journeyed home
Exhausted, but undaunted by the sweat.
Thus smeared with lampsoot, she returned unfazed
To settle odors in the royal pillows.

Ladies of the Night

Claudius returned from his foreign invasion still totally unaware of his wife's indiscretions. Meanwhile, Messalina continued her sexual adventures. Seeking variety, she held orgies where she forced Roman ladies to prostitute themselves with other men and women in front of their husbands. She cuckolded her husband so often that it became a joke in Rome, but by no means was her greed only sexual. One of the profligate Empress' favorite tricks was to make love to men and then learn of their real estate holdings, later condemn them to death for treason, and finally confiscate their property.

However, she went too far when she forced her favorite lover, a handsome youth named Gaius Silius, to divorce his wife and marry her in a public ceremony. The couple celebrated the ceremony by consummating the marriage on a bridal bed that had been placed in full view of their guests. Informed of Messalina's treachery, the Emperor ordered her put to death. She and her lover were stabbed to death by sword in the gardens of Lucullus, which she had obtained by confiscation.

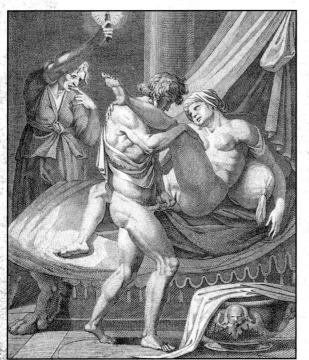

MESSALINE DANS LA LOGE DE LISISCA
Agostino Carracci, 16th century.

Agostino Carracci is known for his erotic engravings from the sixteenth century. This photo is translated literally to "Messalina in Lisisica's Booth," because Messalina was working as a prostitute using the pseudonym Lisisca. Here is her story:

As soon as his wife perceived that her husband was asleep, this august harlot was shameless enough to prefer a common mat to the imperial couch. Assuming night-cowl, and attended by a single maid, she issued forth; then, having concealed her raven locks under a light-coloured peruque, she took her place in a brothel reeking with long-used coverlets. Entering an empty cell reserved for herself, she there took her stand, under the feigned name of Lycisca, her nipples bare and gilded, and exposed to view the womb that bore thee, O nobly-born Britannicus! Here she graciously received all comers, asking from each his fee; and when at length the keeper dismissed his girls, she remained to the very last before closing her cell, and with passion still raging hot within her went sorrowfully away. Then exhausted by men but unsatisfied, with soiled cheeks, and begrimed with the smoke of lamps, she took back to the imperial pillow all the odours of the stews.

Five hundred years later, the Roman Empire was in decline and many of its territories were gone. Africa, Italy, Spain and Rome itself had fallen to the Vandals and Goths. The capitol had shifted to Constantinople, where a long series of Christian emperors ruled. Emperor Justinian, a brilliant general, embodied all the traits of ancient Romans and was determined to restore the empire. In his nearly forty-year rule, he succeeded in a spectacular fashion, reigning over the world's greatest empire.

In a case of Roman history repeating itself, once again the most interesting thing about Emperor Justinian was his wife, Theodora. Born into the lowest of the lower classes, she grew up to become an incredibly beautiful and magnetic woman. Theodora worked as a "dancing girl" and prostitute and was famous for being able to fully satisfy ten men in a single night. She caught the eye of the married Emperor while dancing in the circus. He was so besotted, he changed Roman law that forbade men from the senatorial class from marrying prostitutes. She converted to Christianity, and after the death of his first wife the two were married.

The new empress could very well be considered the first prostitution reformer. She battled valiantly for the welfare of slaves who were sold to bordellos, though the young women were often too afraid of their owners to accuse them. In a former imperial palace she set up a refuge for women who had been forced into the trade, a cloister that existed for centuries. She was a proponent of abortion and enacted a law that punished rapists with death. The first prostitute to become a Roman empress never forgot her origins. She was a champion for those in her old profession and, indeed, all women.

The Politics of Sex in Rome

As I said earlier, there's no doubt that Romans love sex. Though she was never a Lady of the Night, it's likely that these famous Roman women paved the way for such performers as **Cicciolina**, a hardcore porn star who was elected to the Italian parliament, representing a district in Rome, in the late 1980s.

A gorgeous blond woman born Ilona Staller, Cicciolina engaged in group sex, anal sex, and watersports on film. She posed in Playboy, starred with John Holmes in a film about a depraved Roman empress, was the first woman to bare her breasts on Italian television and famously offered to have sex with Saddam Hussein and Osama bin Laden in the interest of peace.

La Dolce Vita! Long live the Roman empire!

VIVE CICCIOLINA!

This photo, taken in 2002, shows former porn star—and now politician, author, and singer—Ilona Staller, A.K.A. Cicciolina, at a book signing in Budapest in 2002.

AP Photo/MTI/Imre Foeldi

The Engagement Ring

In modern marriage ceremonies, rings are generally exchanged. Typically, a diamond engagement ring is first presented to the woman to symbolize commitment, then the couple exchanges wedding bands after the vows are taken. A quick glance at a person's left hand is an easy way to tell whether or not he or she is married—wedding rings are that popular. For much of history men did not wear rings; women did. The trend took off in America during World War II, when troops facing years of separation from their loved ones wore wedding bands as a tangible reminder of a spouse at home.

It is believed that cavemen gave grass or roots to their significant others as a "promise" item. Ancient Egyptians supposedly braided plant sections into circles to signify "immortal love." The Greeks are credited with the belief that the fourth finger on the left hand has a vein ("veina amoris") connected directly to the heart—the reason that men and women today still wear wedding rings on that finger.

Most historians, however, give official credit for wedding rings to the Romans, who usually gave an iron band (to symbolize strength and permanence) to their intended brides to signify love and commitment. However much "love" was involved, the ring also represented a man's distinct "claim" over his woman. The Romans were also the first to engrave their wedding rings with names and dates. For hundreds of years, wedding rings were simple bands, devoid of gemstones.

Pope Nicholas I officially endorsed the idea of engagement rings in the ninth century by making a gold ring a betrothal requirement (a gold ring proved that the man had sufficient means to support a wife). And the first diamond engagement ring in history was given to Mary of Burgundy by the Archduke Maximilian of Hamburg in 1477. Only the very wealthy could afford diamonds, but those who could flaunted their intricate and beautifully designed jewelry.

It took a brilliant advertising and promotions campaign to create mass desire for diamond engagement rings. The De Beers diamond company cleverly went to Hollywood in the 1930s: gifting starlets with huge diamond rings and inserting scenes of ring-shopping couples in movie scripts. As always, the public took its cues from the stars, and diamond engagement rings became an established courtship ritual. The famous De Beers ad campaign "A Diamond Is Forever," which first appeared in 1947, firmly entrenched the idea in the minds of women everywhere. In movies, in magazines, in song: "Diamonds are a girl's best friend."

The diamond is forever. The marriage? Probably not.

CHAPTER ELEVEN

Ladies of the Middle Ages

Spanning a thousand years, the Middle Ages began with the fall of Rome in 496 and ended with the discovery of the New World in 1492. Today we also call the Middle Ages "medieval times" or the "Dark Ages." During this time Europe was a land of lawlessness and violence. It was also home to "the Plague" or "Black Death," which killed off one-third of the entire population—more than twenty-five million people in less than five years. However, it was also a time of some advancement; during this turbulent era, Northern and Western Europe became truly urbanized for the first time.

All medieval men and women in Europe were born Catholic Christians. (The very few outsiders, such as Jews and Moors, were not full citizens.) The idea that clergy led celibate lives was forgotten during the early Middle Ages; debauchery reigned throughout the Catholic Church. This is clearly evident by studying the Gothic architecture of the time. Buildings and cornices were covered in lewd sculptures, with their subjects taken from religious orders: a monk in the middle of intercourse with a woman, an abbot frolicking with several nuns, a naked nun being tormented by monkeys and so on.

Though the Council of Elvira in the fifth century formally excommunicated prostitutes and bawds from the Church, it also contained a provision requiring priests to administer communion to any courtesan who had married a Christian. The Church concerned itself with all matters of life in the Middle Ages, including marriage, divorce, adultery and, yes, prostitution. The business of prostitution was regulated by canon law as well as by individual kingdoms, cities and provinces.

Though many cities and dukedoms forbade prostitution in the neighborhood of churches, it was not uncommon for brothels to be located next door to houses of worship. These brothels were known as "abbeys" and "convents" in the slang of the time, and the Ladies were called "daughters of joy."

Priests and monks were among their best customers. Many areas had laws specifically forbidding brothel-keepers from admitting religious men, though these laws were rarely enforced. When they were, there are accounts of Ladies actually being brought to the monasteries for personal visits! These were medieval outcalls, if you will. No wonder "priest whore" was a common derogatory insult of the time.

Life in the Middle Ages was hard and dangerous. Sanitation and personal cleanliness were unheard of. Plagues frequently swept through and decimated huge parts of the entire population. Official wars and private battles were constantly being fought. The majority of the population was illiterate.

In the small towns and cities, the merchant and craft guilds had many social, religious and protective functions. In most occupations boys were indentured as apprentices for a set period of years to live at a master's house and learn his trade. When the apprenticeship was over, the young man became a journeyman or paid workingman. The ideal was that he would work hard and eventually set himself up in business and become a master. However, the masters determined who could join their ranks and disliked competition; plus, journeyman wages were so

Ladies of the Night

small that few men could ever save any money. This doomed many workingmen in the Middle Ages to a life of bachelorhood, as they could never hope to support a family.

With very few pleasures in life, patronizing prostitutes was one task workingmen in the Middle Ages enjoyed to the fullest. Along with priests, workingmen were a Lady's best customer. Most people considered brothels morally essential and recognized their existence as a necessary fact of life. When city officials wished to recognize a hero or greet an official guest, they often admitted him to the local brothel free of charge. The key to the city once had more than a symbolic meaning!

Although scholars and religious leaders declared prostitutes to be inferior creatures, peasants and workingmen did not agree. Women who worked in brothels were members of a regular guild, paid taxes, had their own patron saints, joined regular citizens in celebrating holy days, and earned a decent living. In public brothels, Ladies of the time were required to do a token amount of work spinning or sewing, but they could escape this obligation by paying a small fine.

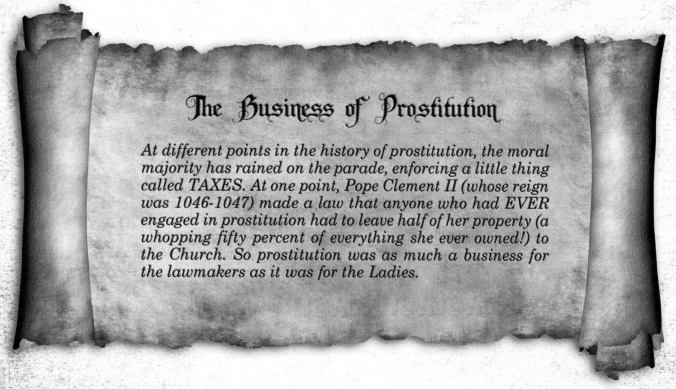

The Business of Prostitution

At different points in the history of prostitution, the moral majority has rained on the parade, enforcing a little thing called TAXES. At one point, Pope Clement II (whose reign was 1046-1047) made a law that anyone who had EVER engaged in prostitution had to leave half of her property (a whopping fifty percent of everything she ever owned!) to the Church. So prostitution was as much a business for the lawmakers as it was for the Ladies.

Patrons were allowed to visit the brothel during the day, though night time, as always, was the busiest time. Here in the brothels a workingman could drink wine, hear music, dance, and enjoy the Lady of his choice. Brothels were officially closed on Sundays and holy days. Given the amount of drinking that went on, it is not surprising that brothels of the Middle Ages were rough, dangerous places. Brawling, stabbing and even murder were not uncommon events.

DETAIL FROM **MERRY COMPANY,** *Braunschweig Monogrammist, ca. 1540*

This tavern scene shows, in amazing detail, various happenings in the interior of a brothel. In the background, we can see the stairs that lead to the rooms upstairs (where Ladies led their prospects for the Night). Debauchery, fighting, sex—this brothel had it all.

Ladies of the Night

It was altogether a rougher time. On the 28th of December, Innocent's Day, men were allowed to enter girls' bedrooms early in the morning. If she was still abed, they were permitted to spank the girl. Of course, matters did not always end with a spanking. Lewd jokes were often told at weddings, and it was a popular amusement of the time to observe through a window or a crack in the wall a newlywed couple in bed consummating their marriage.

The flip side to the bawdiness and rowdiness of medieval times was that the Middle Ages also saw the rise of the feudal system. Valiant men known as knights, skilled in the ways of warfare, protected the serfs and peasants who toiled on their estates. A popular notion took hold: a knight in shining armor worshiped a Lady respectfully from afar, pined for her attention, and performed gallant deeds in her honor. Minstrel poets known as troubadours wrote flowery verses filled with love, fancy language and longing.

Courtly love was quite romantic, but a knight who loved a married woman and acted upon his feelings was in very dangerous territory. Any vassal who made indecent proposals to the wife of his lord was punished by having both hands cut off. And the penalty for a woman could be death. A married, upper-class woman indulging in an adulterous affair was literally endangering her life.

It was during the Middle Ages that the codpiece came into fashion—and men often stuffed them with sawdust to make them appear bigger. Snug-fitting pants were deemed "fashions of the devil" by the church. It was in medieval times that the chastity belt was introduced—a device by which worried husbands could keep their wives' virtue safe by means of lock and key. Chastity was the paramount virtue of high-level married women; it was less a matter of morality than ensuring that huge properties and estates were passed down to legitimate heirs—not bastards.

In fourteenth century France, Philip the Fair discovered that all three of his daughters were having sex with some of his knights. He had the knights disemboweled and the daughters banished to monasteries. Adultery was not a game in those days; the danger was quite real.

France was altogether a harsh place to live during the late Middle Ages. Laws of the time imposed severe penalties upon women convicted of adultery; and prostitution, at least on the books, was punishable by being stoned to death. The laws of Charlemagne, known as the Capitularies, forbade prostitution altogether. Monks were admonished to stop living dissolute lives; nuns were told to stop being "prostitutes, thieves, and murderers." Harlots and bawds (those who frequented prostitutes or were involved in their business dealings) were to be flogged. The Capitularies also attempted to regulate erotic music and dancing.

King Louis VIII made a fruitless effort to control prostitution in the 1200s. Louis IX, powerful and pious, issued an official edict in 1254 ordering the exile of all harlots, brothel-keepers, and bawds. Many women (and men) were thrown into prison or escorted out of France. Those who dared to return to Paris were dealt with so brutally that for two years there was very little prostitution in France.

But the former patrons of brothels simply found women to service them in baths, taverns, and other gathering places. Also, respectable tradesmen complained that it was impossible to maintain the chastity of their wives and daughters under these conditions. The law was repealed, and prostitution came under the control of an official known as The King of Vagabonds. His duties included arresting and punishing any woman who violated official laws pertaining to brothels. He also enforced the new laws that confined prostitution to certain areas of Paris and monitored the laws that forbade Ladies to wear expensive clothing or jewelry. Courtesans were also required to wear badges or ribbons indicating their profession.

Ladies of the Night

.der alt man.

gelt vnd guts gnueg wil ich dir geben . wiltu nach meinem wilen leben.greyff mit d'hãd zu mein taschen das schloß wil-Ich dir erlösen . DES IVNG WEIB Es hilfft kain schlos vir frawen list . Kain trew mag sein da lieb nit ist . darumb Ein schlüssel der mir gfelt . den wil ich kauffen vmv dein gelt • DER IVNG GSEL Ich drag Ein schlüssel zu solchen schlosen . wie wol Es manchen hat verdrosen . der hat der naren kappen vill.der Rocht lieb Erz kauffein wil .   Die ungleichen Liebhaber

CHASTITY BELT, *German woodcut, 16th century*

The poem in this woodcut describes the uselessness of the chastity belt. At one point, the German is translated to:

No lock is of avail against the women of cunning. There can be no fidelity where love is not present. For that reason will I buy with your money the key I lack.

Ladies of the Night cannot be stopped with mere lock and chain.

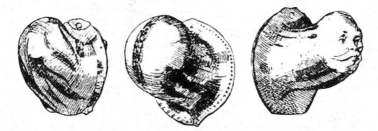

CODPIECES, *Wendelin Boeheim, 16th century*

A strangely delightful illustrated representation of the codpiece.

Penalties for those who disregarded the new laws were extremely severe. Bawds and procuresses were burnt at the stake in thirteenth- and fourteenth-century Paris. Others were forced to stand naked in the city square all day, enduring public whippings and the cutting off of their ears. Mobs delighted in stoning the unfortunate bawds who were found guilty of such crimes as seducing a virgin.

The poems of Francois Villon sum up conditions regarding the French Ladies of the late Middle Ages perfectly: "Happy is he who knows them not."

Prostitution altogether slowed in the late fifteenth century as citizens grew weary of outsiders, strangers, indigents, and foreigners. Respectable people dreaded destitution and the idea

of their own daughters turning to prostitution. Also, the face of prostitution was changing. Far from the bawdy bathhouse girls or common brothel, courtesans would change the face of prostitution.

PORTRAIT OF KARL V (1500-58) OF HABSBURG
Tiziano Vecellio, 1532-3

A medieval man's best friends: dog and codpiece.

CHAPTER TWELVE

Native American Ladies

❧

*B*eginning in the early 1500s, the Spanish Church sent soldiers of the feared and dreaded Inquisition across the Atlantic Ocean to conquer the New World. They landed in what is now Mexico and there encountered the indigenous people of the land, the Mayan Indians.

The Spanish believed the Mayans to be savages—perhaps because of their religious rituals involving blood sacrifice, particularly to the god of maize. In reality they had a flourishing culture and a very balanced view of sexuality. A polygamous society, the Mayans believed that sex was a necessary and life-affirming pleasure, but also an activity to be undertaken in moderation. Too much sex with too many partners—promiscuity on the part of either a man or a woman—indicated lack of control and would invoke the wrath of various gods. Adultery was punishable by death. Ritual murder of adulterers was accomplished by smashing in the adulterer's head with rocks until that person was dead. According to ancient Mayan law, he who courted or made signs to a married woman was banished from the tribe forever.

The natives worshipped deities in addition to the all-important god of maize (corn). Naturally, there was a goddess of love and fertility, in following with the cultural practices of many other ancient civilizations. Nina was one of their goddesses, queen of heaven and ruler of the cycles of the seasons and fertility. She was the widely known goddess in the later periods of summer, the warmer time of the year, which encourages sexual activity. She was represented with a fish tail or serpent tail (also having sexual connotations) and was associated with herbs, the moon, healing, magic, intercession, and interpretation of dreams, crops, and civilization.

Being explicitly a goddess of sexuality and fertility, her worship included sacred prostitution. With wings and serpents adorning her shoulders, we can see a trace of the ancient neolithic bird and snake goddess. The symbol of caduceus staff and the double-headed axe both represent her power to bestow and withdraw life, which made her a very powerful role model. She indeed had it all: sensuality, political skills, intelligence, beauty and power. She was aware of her prostitution in the world and knew the great responsibility she had to fulfill.

The Spanish disdained the worship of pagan gods but were more concerned with gold than religion. It took less than 100 years to wipe out the Mayan empire. Then the conquerors moved on to the Aztecs. While similar to the Mayan culture in many ways, the Aztecs were more of a proud warrior race. They practiced human sacrifice and cannibalism. They, too, approached sex with a balanced view, though the Spanish exaggerated their strange religious and sex practices in order to justify their wholesale murder and plunder of the Aztec civilization. Accusing them of sodomy gave the Spanish invaders all the justification they needed to conquer them.

Ladies of the Night

AZTEC WOMAN BLOWING ON MAIZE (CORN) BEFORE PUTTING IT INTO THE COOKING POT, ca. late 16th century

MAYAHUEL—AZTEC GODDESS OF ALCOHOL, Edinburgh University Press, 1902

Mayahuel, according to Aztec mythology, was a human god whom the wind god fell in love with. So she could express love for him in return, he gave the human race the gift of love. As sweet as that sounds, Mayahuel became the goddess of the maguey plant in addition to fertility. Because Mayahuel drank so much of the alcoholic drink made by the maguey, the breasts from which her many, many children drank supposedly are the root of all drunkenness in the world.

The ancient Aztec/Mexican goddess Tlazolteotl was the goddess of love and sexuality whose worship included sacred prostitution. In her dark aspect she is associated with witchcraft and terror—which probably didn't help her out in the sex department. The rituals honoring her—involving death and human sacrifice—are part of what gave the Aztecs their terrifying bloodthirsty reputation. Still, she had a benign side and was as much loved as she was feared. Tlazolteotl was Matron of both pleasure and sin, though not in the sense many Christians would think. Her name translates in English to mean "Filth Deity." In the Aztec mind, sex was unclean (hence the filth-y name) yet fertility was prided among the ancient Aztec people.

Aztecs had their own group of prostitutes, "pleasure women" or "merry women" they were called. They held a respected place in Aztec society and played a role in the religious ceremonies, freely mingling with the most respected elders of the tribe.

Another group of women was not so highly regarded. Lower-class prostitutes plied their trade along the canals of Tenochtitlan, so the Spanish referred to them as women of the water. These women painted their faces red, dyed their teeth and styled their hair in a distinctive manner in order to distinguish themselves from the more virtuous women. The Spaniards spoke and wrote of these women in very derogatory terms but certainly sampled their services.

The Aztec civilization was at its zenith in 1519 when Spanish conquistador Hernán Cortés captured the ruler Montezuma. The most notorious woman of precolonial Mexico, La Malinche—or Doña Marina, as she was known by the Spanish conquistadores—was at his side. A brilliant Aztec woman with remarkable language skills, she had been sold into slavery, learned Spanish in just a few weeks, and became the interpreter, adviser, and eventually mistress of Cortés during his expeditions and the ultimate conquest of Tenochitlan. Although she has been reviled by scholars and her people as a collaborator, modern female historians have been resurrecting the reputation of La Malinche,

Ladies of the Night

noting that she deliberately (and wisely) used the influence she came to wield over Cortés (i.e., SEX!) to save the lives of thousands of Native Indians.

Cortés had discovered the weakness of the new Native American Empire: that it was nothing more than a collection of smaller groups of people (tribes) who were tied together by one thing: membership in this society. Many of these communities despised the Aztecs and wanted freedom from their rule. Cortés exploited this desire to its fullest. By gathering up more than 150,000 of these natives and 9,000 of his own troops, he completely dismantled the Aztec Empire—in the process gaining control of those who were fighting for their own freedom. When a devastating smallpox epidemic wiped out half the city of Tenochtitlan, Cortés seized the city and laid it in ruins. By August 13, 1521, the Aztec empire was gone forever, and Spanish rule soon spread throughout the newly gained land.

The Spaniards had used the native religious and sexual differences as an excuse to destroy two ancient civilizations, condemning them as uncivilized savages to people back home only too willing to believe any tale of their debauchery and ignorance.

La Malinche and Hernán Cortés in the city of Xaltelolco, *late 16th century*

La Malinche was an indigenous woman from Mexico who accompanied Hernán Cortés and played an active and powerful role in the Spanish conquest of Mexico.

CHAPTER THIRTEEN

The Courtesans of

Europe's Renaissance

The European Renaissance (French for "rebirth") refers to a period of some 300 years, roughly covering from 1300 to 1600. The Renaissance cultural movement began in Italy and soon spread throughout Europe. It was marked by a return to classical learning, sparking unpredecented achievements in education, science, literature, philosophy, politics, and particularly the arts. Leonardo Da Vinci and Michelangelo are both credited with inspiring the term "renaissance man" for their amazing artistic works.

In Italy (and to a lesser degree, Spain, France and the Netherlands) a whole body of literature is devoted to the Renaissance courtesan. An enduring image of the "honest courtesan" emerged at this time, and the writers, painters and poets of the time have left vivid impressions of this important female figure. In literature, Pietro Aretino produced a major treatise on the courtesan in the form of a bawdy social satire in deliberately plebian language. In the world of art, priceless paintings immortalizing courtesans now hang in museums and reflect the beauty and fashion standards of the time.

GABRIELLE D'ESTREES WITH HER SISTER, Author Unknown, 1594

Gabrielle d'Estrees (1571-1599) was a mistress of King Henry IV of France. Although Henry was obviously married to another woman, he and his mistress were not afraid to publicly display their affection for each other. Many of the French elite did not approve of Henry's other "Lady" so they nicknamed her various things, including "Duchess of Filth."

In this painting, Gabrille d'Estrees is wearing a ring that Henry gave her. Although the painting seems to give off a homosexual vibe (between Gabrielle and her sister, no less!) it is actually expressing her forthcoming birth (some believe Cesar, the son that she would have with King Henry). Her sister pinches her nipple, where the new mother's milk will come. The fireplace in the center of the piece represents the mother's "furnace."

Ladies of the Night

It was commonplace at the time to remark that Renaissance-era Rome was one vast brothel. According to the 1490 census, there were more than 6,800 prostitutes in Rome, out of a population of less than 50,000. For one thing, men vastly outnumbered women, an ideal situation for women to ply this ancient trade. Furthermore, a French writer and traveler in the sixteenth century wrote that "Roman ladies copulate like bitches but are silent as stones." All the powerful men of the time—merchants, bankers, those in the papal court—were anxious to live *la dolce vita*, and the wives were not fulfilling their needs. They did not want a common prostitute; it was not just sex they sought. Gentlemanly manners, respect for women and gallantry were in fashion for noblemen of the Renaissance, and women were able to take advantage of their new emotional refinement. It was during the Renaissance that notions of romantic love came into being. It was the time of star-crossed lovers and longing and finding one's destined soul mate; hence the flowering of the courtesan.

A select group of smart women saw the advantages of positioning themselves as objects of desire and luxury, available as suitable companions for high-placed men. They schooled themselves in every art of fine living, realizing that they had to be clean, impeccably dressed, cunning at card and board games, able to sing and play an instrument, recite poetry from memory, and converse intelligently about the political issues of the day in two or three languages. These beautiful and elegant women were completely different from common prostitutes, honored and respected by the powerful men of the time. In the sixteenth century, the Roman courtesans enjoyed their Golden Age.

PORTRAIT OF MADAME DE POMPADOUR, François Boucher, ca. 1750

Madame de Pompadour, the hot young thing in the above portrait, was a famous courtesan and mistress of Louis XV of France. Like many courtesans before her, she was smart, beautiful, and had a well-to-do background. By the time she was twenty-three, she had considerable influence, presiding over interior design as well as politics in the royal court. To silence any who might think the King did not treat Pompadour as well as she deserved, he remained in love with her even after her death; and even four years after they stopped having sex!

Ladies of the Night

Imperia, the most famous courtesan of the time, lived in a home that "if one judged by the splendid furnishings and number of servants, one might think a princess lived in that palace." In her bedroom hung tapestries woven of pure gold, with walls inlaid with precious stones. In the center of her salon were musical instruments, scores and valuable works of literature which rested on a velvet-covered table, giving dazzled visitors to her chambers the impression of culture and opulence. She invented black silk bed-sheets, liking the contrast they provided against her pale naked skin.

Veronica Franco, the mistress of two famous painters, Tintoretto and Veronese, served as their model, spoke seven languages, wrote poetry, set fashion trends, and was the only woman of her time who managed to seduce King Henri III of France (he preferred men but was overcome by her beauty). One kiss from Veronica would cost the average Venetian worker six months' wages.

The daughter of a prostitute and a Cardinal, Tuillia d'Aragonza was fortunate that her father acknowledged paternity and paid for her excellent education. As a beautiful young courtesan, Tuillia became famous for throwing the most lavish parties Rome had ever seen, attended by the Medici popes and all of Rome's nobility. She made a grave misstep by openly favoring a rich German client over Rome's aristocracy. Her German lover left, and just like that, Tuillia became the object of a vicious whisper campaign and was soon hounded out of town.

After being chased all over Italy, from Ferrara to Venice to Tuscany, Tuillia returned some years later and was humiliated by the new pope, Paul III, who forced her to wear a veil in public, the sign of a common prostitute. Her last years were spent wandering the streets of the city she once had at her feet.

An interesting footnote: The sumptuous clothes the courtesans wore and the furnishings for their magnificent homes were rented from Jews, from whom they were forbidden by law to bestow their favors, though many did anyway.

The Jews of Italy's Renaissance were only allowed to live in the "getta"—the place outside the city where bricks were baked in smoke-filled buildings—hence our modern word "ghetto." The original ghettos were Jewish ghettos. Despite their poverty and poor living conditions, industrious Jews were the lifeline for every courtesan's glamorous outfits.

How did a courtesan actually conduct business? In a description of the time, Banedello describes:

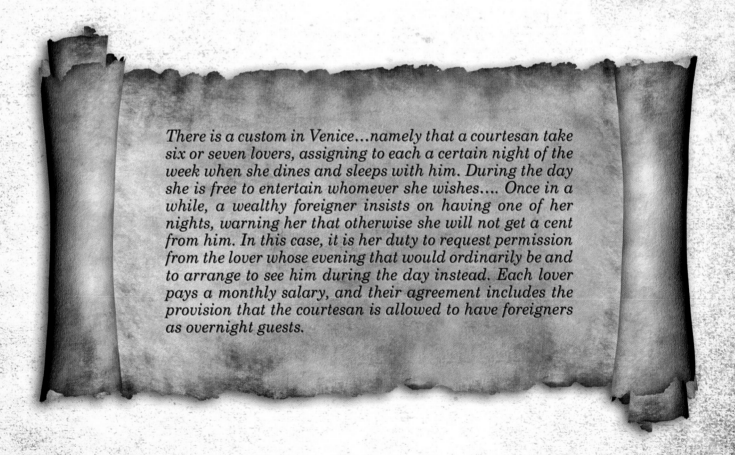

There is a custom in Venice…namely that a courtesan take six or seven lovers, assigning to each a certain night of the week when she dines and sleeps with him. During the day she is free to entertain whomever she wishes…. Once in a while, a wealthy foreigner insists on having one of her nights, warning her that otherwise she will not get a cent from him. In this case, it is her duty to request permission from the lover whose evening that would ordinarily be and to arrange to see him during the day instead. Each lover pays a monthly salary, and their agreement includes the provision that the courtesan is allowed to have foreigners as overnight guests.

Ladies of the Night

The Ladies of the Renaissance were witty, fun, and unashamed of their profession. Isabella de Luna, who had once been a lowly camp follower servicing several armies (called by the French a *marketenderin*—marcher-into-the-tent), eventually retired to Rome in the mid-1500s and took a lover from a prominent Florentine banking family. He advised his mistress on all financial and real estate matters, and Isabella eventually acquired her own building in Rome and collected rents from her tenants.

At a dinner party full of nobles one night, the guests played an early version of Truth or Dare, and a spiteful cardinal in attendance, well aware of Isabella's history, challenged her to reveal her sordid past to the entire gathering—going so far as to hand her a written summary of her life including every salacious detail. "What can you say about me other than I am a whore? Everyone knows it already; there is no need to blush about it!" the unfazed Lady told the guests.

Instead of reading her own story, Isabella launched into an impromptu but devastating account of the Cardinal's life—his sharp tongue and malicious gossip had earned him many enemies. The Cardinal left the party in shame, and Isabella continued to enjoy her evening.

And the beautiful Veronica of Venice, subject of history's greatest painters, whose kiss would cost a regular worker six months' wages? When one of her lovers became angry at her and verbally abused her, she eloquently defended herself: "If you insist on calling me a whore, that is all right, for if I am one, there must be praiseworthy ones in the world!"

She was correct; many of the Renaissance Ladies were praiseworthy indeed.

LA VIOLANTE, *Palma Vecchio, 16th century*

A beautiful Renaissance-era courtesan.

MARS UNDRESSING VENUS, *Veronese, 16th century*

Venetian Renaissance painter Veronese is behind this great work showcasing Venus, a name associated in Roman history with love, beauty, and fertility. Venus was almost always pictured nude (it was her natural state) and, as a goddess representing pure and unadulterated sexuality, she was usually portrayed erotically. Over time, "Venus" has become associated with any nude, post-classical art.

CHAPTER FOURTEEN

Ladies of the Victorian Age

Many Puritans, who were quite unhappy with the Church of England, packed up and headed to the New World in great numbers out of sheer disgust at the excesses of European life in the seventeenth and eighteenth centuries. But in the mid-1800s a young queen exemplified a new way of life that quickly swept through the British Empire, especially the growing middle class. Victorians, as they were called, turned their backs on the immorality and debauchery of the aristocrats of previous generations—they preferred to live a moral life.

Seventeen-year-old Queen Victoria of Germany took the English throne in 1837. A pure and virginal maiden, Victoria fell in love at first sight with her cousin Albert, and married him shortly afterward. Albert was not a political choice but one from her heart, and they remained devoted to each other until his sudden death twenty years later. The royal couple reigned over the expanding British Empire but also centered their lives around their nine children and many pets, thereby resurrecting the ideal of romantic love in marriage and the pleasures of home and hearth.

The concept of the "honeymoon" arose in Victorian times. The pleasure trip immediately after the wedding was a symbol of the separation of the young couple from their families for the first time, as well as a time of their sexual initiation. Young women and men of Victorian times, especially those from middle- and upper-class families, had very little sexual knowledge or know-how.

Many newlyweds were both virgins on the wedding day, though the lower and working classes took a more tolerant view of pre-marital sex. For middle- and upper-class men, any premarital sex would have been with servants and prostitutes, since "nice girls" looking to marry didn't venture beyond a kiss on the cheek or brief hand-holding. It was a tradition throughout Victorian England for upper-class men to have their initial sexual experiences with prostitutes, the first of which typically took place while they were away at universities. These men received little more than a reprimand if caught by the authorities.

Once legally wed and home from the honeymoon, a marriage in Victorian times was generally very traditional. The husband worked and provided; the wife managed the home and raised children. Sex was not freely discussed at the time, even between husband and wife. It was considered a normal and desirable urge, but only condoned under the proper circumstances: between a married couple, for the purpose of procreation. Adultery in Victorian times, particularly by a woman, was out of the question.

A leading physician of the era, Dr. William Acton, was an advocate of the "frigid wife" ideal of the time. Mothers and wives were supposed to feel passion only for their children, cooking, and upkeep of their home. They submitted to their husbands to please them, not to gain any sense of pleasure. With young women remaining virgins until marriage and wives ignorant of all sexual matters and expected only to submit, there was an explosion of prostitution in Victorian England.

There were about 80,000 "gay" women (prostitutes) and "fancy men" (pimps) in London in the mid-nineteenth century. They congregated around Covent Garden and in the theater district. The Ladies tucked part of their skirts up to indicate their availability and were especially tempting to soldiers, most of whom were forbidden to marry. London at this time was

Ladies of the Night

frequently referred to as "the whoreshop of the world," though it had relatively few official brothels. Most business was done in rooming houses whose owners looked the other way while the Ladies who lived there conducted their business.

It is impossible to estimate the number of "occasional" prostitutes, called "dollymops," who supplemented their meager earnings as dressmakers or milliners with occasional acts of sex for pay. Some nineteenth-century observers believed that these part-time, casual prostitutes greatly exceeded the more visible, full-time streetwalkers.

The typical London prostitute was young, came from a rural area, and found herself on her own in the big city. She could be found in the city's many pubs, which no respectable Victorian woman would enter. Often unskilled and suited only for low-wage jobs such as maids, these young women turned to prostitution as the best way to earn money in the city. Many worked as Ladies only for a short time—often turning a favorite client into a husband. Once married and settled, the Ladies became regular middle-class wives and mothers.

Sailors were a large customer base for both official and part-time Ladies. These women would often become close to their customers, spending several nights at a time with them while they were on shore leave and entrusted to hold money for the sailors while they were away at sea. One Lady of the time described it such: "I know very many sailors—six, eight, ten, oh! More than that. They are my husbands. I am not married, of course not, but they think me their wife while they are on shore." *That's* my kind of marriage!

Most Victorian cities—not just London—had at least one notorious district where public women lived and plied their trade among a wide cross-section of the working class. Some districts were traditional centers of prostitution, like the Walter Lanes of York. They all acquired derogatory nicknames, such as "Grapecunt Lane" in York, the "Dust-Hole" in Greenwich, and "Damnation Alley" in Plymouth.

On the whole, prostitution in Victorian Britain was a trade largely organized by women rather than men. In fact, a strong female subculture was a distinguishing feature of nineteenth-century prostitution. Power to the Ladies of the Night! Even though prostitution appeared to operate in an arena of male supremacy, the reality in Victorian times was that women often controlled the business. Ladies also tended to live together as part of a distinct female subgroup. They could act in their own defense, negotiate their own prices, and even exploit their customers.

As "outcast women," the Ladies stuck together and adopted an outward appearance and more affluent style of life to distinguish themselves from other working-class women. The most visible symbol of the prostitute's relative affluence was her dress. Middle-class citizens frequently complained about the "painted dressy women flaunted along the streets" in "dirty white muslin and greasy cheap blue silk." This dress code also served as their way of advertising themselves and attracting male customers, just as it does today. Bonnet-less, without shawls, they presented themselves "in their figure" to any and all passersby. What respectable Victorian women saw as shameless flaunting no doubt signified status and freedom from the drudgery of the workaday world for Victorian Ladies.

The entire system operated, as did everything else in Victorian England, on the class system. The highest tier of Ladies was comprised of the courtesans and mistresses, often set up in their own separate, second households. Even Charles Dickens, a pillar of Victorian morals, kept a mistress for twenty years. (His mistress later married a minister and led a circumspect middle-class life.)

Then there were brothels. Some were high-class, elegant establishments that functioned much like exclusive private clubs. Others that catered to the working class were less fancy. Specialized houses were all the rage in Victorian England—they specialized in satisfying certain desires, such as bondage,

Ladies of the Night

humiliation, or discipline. In the 1870s Mary Jeffries ran an exclusive brothel serving the aristocracy, with one of her rooms outfitted like a torture chamber for sado-masochistic sex. It had rings extending from the ceiling to hang clients by their wrists, and every imaginable kind of whip, including branches and cat o' nine tails.

One of the great scandals of the Victorian age was the fact that impoverished families were known to sell their children into specialized brothels that featured young virgins. The higher the social class of the child, the higher their price, with an upper-class girl under the age of twelve bringing the highest price. A journalist ignited a scandal in 1885 when he purchased the services of a thirteen-year-old virgin, just to demonstrate how easily it could be done. Tremendous moral outrage occurred; the official age of consent was later changed by law to the age of sixteen.

Despite the morals of the age, there was seemingly little public censure for most of this type of behavior in Victorian England. Homosexuality, not prostitution, was the ultimate taboo, culminating in the trial and imprisonment of the great writer and humorist Oscar Wilde in 1895.

The decline of Victorian ethics ended at the turn of the new century. Queen Victoria died in 1901, still wearing black and having mourned her husband for forty years. With the death of the era's namesake, the age remembered today mainly for its prudishness and quaint morals came to an end.

A HARLOT'S PROGRESS, PLATE 3, William Hogarth, 1732
"Moll, in debt, is prosecuted by Sir John Gonson,
a whore-hunter of the period."

William Hogarth is a famous English artist, known for his engraving series' "A Harlot's Progress" and "A Rake's Progress." "A Harlot's Progress" tells the story of a young woman named Mary, who comes to the big city of London and becomes a prostitute. When she first arrives in town, an old woman tells her how pretty she is and points her in the direction of the gentlemen. After becoming the mistress of several lovers, she spirals downward and ends up dying of a venereal disease. Although it's not exactly an uplifting tale, there was a good moral for the Ladies of the eighteenth century: Use protection!

Ladies of the Night

A Rake's Progress, Plate 8, William Hogarth, 1735
"In the Madhouse."

This series of engravings tells the story of Tom, who receives a large inheritance from his dead father. He then proceeds to spend all of that money, mostly on prostitutes and gambling and partying. In this final scene, he is in the famous Bethlehem Hospital in London—Bedlam—where women still surround him, this time to watch him suffer!

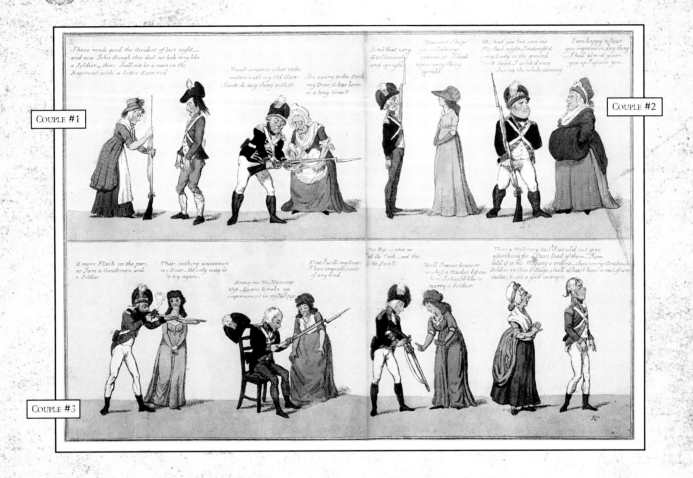

"FEMALE OPINIONS ON MILITARY TACTICS" Isaac Cruikshank, 1790s

The Male/Female Dichotomy: Not much has changed!

COUPLE #1 Husband—I can't conceive what is the matter with my Old Gun. I can't do anything with it!
Wife—It's owing to the Cock, my Dear; it has been so a long time!

COUPLE #2 Man—Is not that very Gentlemanly and upright?
Young Lady—Yes, and I hope you will always continue so. I doat upon everything upright.

COUPLE #3 Husband—Bring me the Hammer, Wife. I want to make an improvement in my Tailpipe.
Wife—That I will, my Dear; I love improvements of any kind.

CHAPTER FIFTEEN
Ladies of the
Wild, Wild West

Meanwhile, across the Atlantic Ocean, if you were truly a refined Lady (in the original sense of the word) in the American West, you most likely wouldn't be living there at all. Only civilized cities out West like San Francisco had department stores with pretty clothes and beauty salons, where a woman could dress properly and appear appropriately ladylike. The many women who wound up making a living in the gold rush towns during the 1850s were literally there seeking their own gold.

The dancing girls and saloon hall girls we've all seen so many times in the movies were prostitutes! In Wild West saloons, men drank downstairs, and a girl would always come by to keep them company. Then they took her upstairs to have some fun. These good-time girls came out West in droves and welcomed prospectors and settlers with open arms and open legs. The only people unhappy about this were the few "respectable" women in town: the men's wives and girlfriends. The business of selling sex had plenty to do with opening the gateway to the West. It is an amazing but true fact that more than half of all working women in the West during the 1870s were prostitutes.

Prostitution boomed in all the urban areas in the years 1865-90. Obviously, the larger the urban community, the greater the potential for disparity in the standard of living for prostitutes. Working as a "sporting woman" or "soiled dove," as they were called, was a profession for the young. A Wild West Lady's age ranged from seventeen to twenty-five (although there are a few cases of younger and older Ladies, no one over the age of twenty-eight could make a living selling sex). As their moneymaking services were really only viable at a young age, most soiled doves spent just a few years "in the life."

In the West, like every other culture throughout history, there were different classes of prostitutes: here, depending on her location and her clientele. The high-class prostitutes worked in parlor houses, which were grand and beautiful mansions. These high-class Ladies could earn more than twenty-five dollars a night, most of which went into the hands of the madam who, in return, used much of it for the upkeep of the parlor house.

The lowest class of Western whores were the crib women and streetwalkers. "Cribs," common throughout frontier communities, were small structures, usually clustered together in an alley or along a roadway. Some were flimsy shacks with only space for a cot and a chair, while others were built of brick or adobe and remain tourist attractions today. The easy accessibility, lack of protection, and bleak locations of the cribs made this category of work just a small step above the lowly streetwalker. When women slipped into these categories, it meant almost surely a permanent demotion.

Western Ladies' "place of business" had a variety of names, including "the half world," "the badlands," "the tenderloin," "the twilight zone," or "the red-light district." Some historians claim that the term "red-light district" originated in Kansas. To discourage intruders, railroad workers around Dodge City would hang their red lanterns outside their doors as a signal that they were in the company of a Lady of the Night. The madams and their Ladies quickly adopted this tradition, and the name stuck.

The most infamous Ladies of the Wild West tend to be known by their nicknames and aliases. This is because they

Ladies of the Night

changed their names frequently to avoid getting caught by the law. The real, official names of many of the prostitutes and madams catering to the sexual appetites of outlaws, cowboys, miners, soldiers and muleskinners went unrecorded. Their pseudonyms, however, were quite descriptive.

"Contrary Mary," "Spanish Queen," "Little Gold Dollar," "Em Straight Edge," "Peg Leg Annie," and "Molly B'Damned" (who, interestingly, quoted Shakespeare, Milton and Dante for her patrons) were just a few of the more colorful Ladies of the West.

And who is the most famous Lady of all in the Wild West? Calamity Jane, formerly known as Martha Jane Cannary. No beauty, the tough, mannish-looking Lady was further ravaged by years of drinking and hard living. At twenty-four she had already been working the West for eight years, moving from town to town. Her fame is mostly due to her friendship with Wild Bill Hickok, whom she claimed was her lover. As ravaged as she may have been, the eccentric woman managed to outlive Wild Bill. The man famous throughout the West for his quick-draw was gunned down while playing poker at Nuttal and Man's Saloon

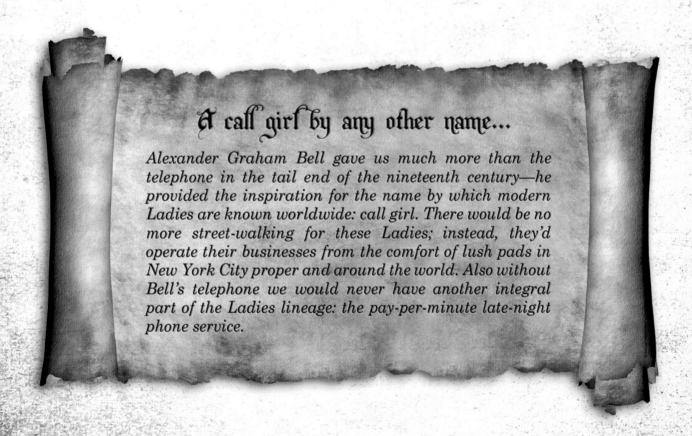

A call girl by any other name...

Alexander Graham Bell gave us much more than the telephone in the tail end of the nineteenth century—he provided the inspiration for the name by which modern Ladies are known worldwide: call girl. There would be no more street-walking for these Ladies; instead, they'd operate their businesses from the comfort of lush pads in New York City proper and around the world. Also without Bell's telephone we would never have another integral part of the Ladies lineage: the pay-per-minute late-night phone service.

No. 10 in Deadwood, South Dakota. He was holding aces and eights, forever-after known as the Dead Man's Hand.

Calamity Jane's dying words were a request to be buried next to him. After the biggest funeral ever seen in Deadwood, her final wish was granted. Ironically, as he was the love of her life, Bill considered Calamity Jane a pain and never once had sex with her. Still, she is buried next to him for all eternity.

CALAMITY JANE, Photo by H.R. Locke, 1895

Calamity Jane, born Martha Jane Cannary, was nothing short of a bad ass—and looked it. This gun-totin' chick won the heart of infamous Wild Bill Hickok (although supposedly it was more a "friends only" type of relationship—despite claims from Jane that she gave birth to Hickok's child). Hickok and Jane met in Deadwood, South Dakota, home of some of the most notorious Wild West brothels.

Ladies of the Night

Entertainment in the now-infamous town of Deadwood was described as such: Not every bar had prostitutes, but every house of prostitution had a bar. In rough Western towns like Deadwood, where men far outnumbered women, the possibility for an unmarried woman to find a husband was high. The temptation to sell sex was equally high. Kitty Leroy, like many Ladies of the time, tried both.

Kitty packed a lot of living into her twenty-eight years. Originally from Texas, Kitty was a professional gambler and part-time dancer/Lady who had run through four husbands by the time she arrived in Deadwood and opened the Mint Gambling Saloon. Her husband, Curley, while not bothered by her profession, became unhinged over rumors of her affairs with the outlaw Sam Bass and the famous Wild Bill. He burst into her rooming house, raced up the stairs to her second-floor room, and shot her, then himself. Afterwards, the saloon owner/madam of the house washed off the blood, powdered Kitty's face, and made her look as sexy as she had been in life for her "laying-out."

All of the real saloon girls of the Wild West tended to be very tough cookies. They not only had sex for money but drank and smoked (unheard-of for women to do in those more "proper" times) and were not averse to "rolling" a drunken customer and relieving him of his cash. These women were also the owners and madams of many of the brothels and saloons, and did whatever they had to in order to survive. The Wild West was no place for the faint of heart—man or woman.

Native American women came into the Wild West picture of prostitution. Some historical sources claim that Native American women enjoyed considerable freedom in the old days. It was actually considered an advantage if a woman was not a virgin when she chose a husband. "Free women" were praised in Native American culture—as they should be! The Navajos, for instance, let free women set up their tents and entertain the men as they wished. Several other tribes in Mexico, Nevada, and Texas were documented as having practiced prostitution as well. In the

Sierra Tarasca tribe, there were even older women who acted as "madams" and set up agreements for the younger women of the tribe to exchange their sex for money.

Indian tribes in the early 1800s offered their women to the sailors who arrived on the California coast. As Indian women lost respect in the eyes of Puritan women, prostitution proliferated, since it was no longer socially acceptable for white men to marry Indian women. The most frequent customers were "the boys in blue," or soldiers, who were stationed at military forts in between the Indian reservations and the remaining wilderness.

Prostitution was simply a fact of life throughout the West, and the Ladies of the Night prospered (during all hours of the day, actually). But Western towns, determined to exercise a certain degree of supervision over these Ladies, made sure that they remained relatively segregated from respectable citizens. Lawmakers heavily regulated and taxed them in order to control their activities. The tax money taken in from these women often became a major source of their communities' incomes and paid for schools and other public facilities, lessening the tax burden on the "good" people of the town. Little, therefore, was done to actually remove members of the world's oldest profession from their midst.

Still, there were plenty of people who didn't care for the Ladies. As opposition to the ill-reputed profession grew, supporters made their voices heard, as one miner expressed in his poem published in a 1901 Colorado newspaper:

> *There is so much bad in the best of us.*
> *And so much good in the worst of us.*
> *That it hardly behooves any of us*
> *To talk about the rest of us.*

And one of the most hilarious writings of the time was an official notice hung in Arizona in 1882, by a Sheriff "Doc" Linton:

Ladies of the Night

All women of dubious character in the fair city of Tombstone must continue to confine themselves to the shady side of the street. This applies particularly to Amazon Amy, Big-Nosed Bertha, Bubbles Berrick, Footsie Ferrel, Formaldehyde Flo, Coal Oil Katie, Fifi L'Amour, Tuberculosis Tessie, Toothy Jane, and twenty others. You all know who this concerns. If any of you are seen on the sunny side of the street, there's a quiet place waiting for you—jail. The alternative is to leave town for good. At any rate that would be good for Tombstone.

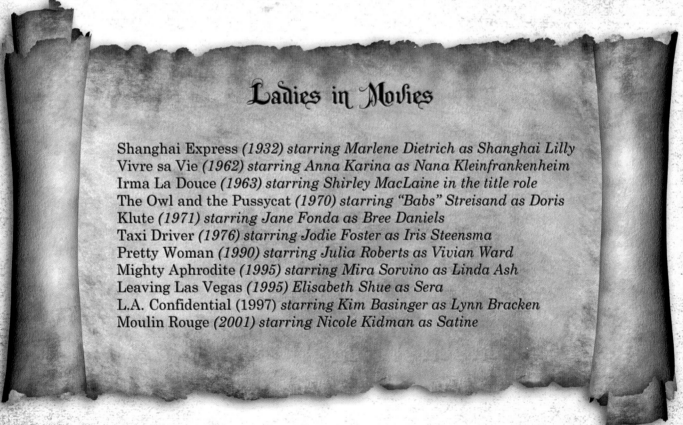

Ladies in Movies

Shanghai Express *(1932) starring Marlene Dietrich as Shanghai Lilly*
Vivre sa Vie *(1962) starring Anna Karina as Nana Kleinfrankenheim*
Irma La Douce *(1963) starring Shirley MacLaine in the title role*
The Owl and the Pussycat *(1970) starring "Babs" Streisand as Doris*
Klute *(1971) starring Jane Fonda as Bree Daniels*
Taxi Driver *(1976) starring Jodie Foster as Iris Steensma*
Pretty Woman *(1990) starring Julia Roberts as Vivian Ward*
Mighty Aphrodite *(1995) starring Mira Sorvino as Linda Ash*
Leaving Las Vegas *(1995) Elisabeth Shue as Sera*
L.A. Confidential (1997) *starring Kim Basinger as Lynn Bracken*
Moulin Rouge *(2001) starring Nicole Kidman as Satine*

CHAPTER SIXTEEN

Ladies of New Orleans

*N*ew Orleans, the most European city in America, has always enjoyed the reputation of a city where anything goes, sexually or otherwise. Its motto, after all, is *Laissez les bon temps roulez*…let the good times roll.

In the 1700 and 1800s in this young city, men greatly outnumbered women, making the Big Easy a hotbed of prostitution and a place where sex across the color lines was both commonplace and acceptable. Attempts by early reformers in the mid-1800s to regulate brothels were unsuccessful; after much debate, it was decided that such change would be against the public good. After that it was full speed ahead: brothels and sex-related businesses proliferated all over the city.

In 1897 a businessman named Sidney Story proposed a law that all prostitutes must live and conduct business within a certain proscribed area. His reasoning was that by containing all such business in a small area, the entire city would not be seen as so debauched—nor would the various neighborhoods in the city suffer loss of property values because brothels were springing up all around them. His idea backfired; having all the sex businesses in one concentrated area made New Orleans even more famous for prostitution. Much to the businessman's dismay, the new area of town, which would eventually encompass twenty-square-blocks just north and west of the French Quarter, was called Storyville.

Tom Anderson, the unofficial "Mayor of Storyville," got his start by running errands for two famous madams. Eventually he founded his own brothel, called Anderson Annex—later renamed Arlington Annex after his lover Josie Arlington. He also owned a restaurant and saloon in the area and soon became the area's unofficial political boss. (He died in 1931 after finding salvation in religion and giving up his wicked ways, though he left a sizeable estate from all his Storyville profits.)

ADVERTISEMENT FROM THE "BLUE BOOK" printed between 1904-17

This is an advertisement for Josie Arlington's high-rent brothel in New Orlean's own Storyville. "Blue Books" were guides to the prostitution district that were published between 1895 and 1915; they gave customers house descriptions, a list of services, and prices. They also all had the same inscription inside: "Order of the Garter: Honi Soit Qui Mal Y Pense [Evil to Him Who Evil Thinks.]"

Ladies of the Night

Prostitution in Storyville was strongly influenced by New Orleans' long history of interracial sex between white men and black women. Race played a major role in determining a Lady's price. Octoroons—a woman who was one-eighth African-American and seven-eighths white—were the most highly prized, with several houses in Storyville staffed only with octoroons, who commanded a very high price. It's interesting that at this time and place, many white women actually passed themselves off as having African-American blood to make more money.

Lulu Wright was Storyville's most famous octoroon madam. Well, she called herself that, but she was more likely the daughter of sharecroppers, though she reinvented herself in New Orleans as so many did. Known as Queen of the Diamonds, she wore as many diamonds as she could possibly fit on her hands, wrists and around her neck.

Her Mahogany Hall was the ultimate in luxury, with fine art, wallpaper, crystal chandeliers and Jelly Roll Morton playing the piano in the lounge. Men leaving her palace were given a feather for their hat or a pin for their lapel, a sign to the rest of the businesses in Storyville that this man had already been taken care of for the night. A souvenir from Lulu meant that the man was spent.

Hattie Hamilton was another famous madam of Storyville. In 1870, she shot one of her clients, Mr. David Jackson, a Louisiana senator, in his home. Such was her influence that she was released by the police without being charged or even questioned. Kate Townsend, another famous madam, was not so lucky. She was killed by her lover Troisville Sykes in 1883. He pleaded self-defense, was released, and despite the circumstances inherited her ninety-thousand-dollar fortune. Clearly New Orleans' prostitutes and their madams made a very good living.

The wonderful music New Orleans is famous for got a big boost from a tradition that began in Storyville. The best bordellos each hired a house pianist universally known as "The Professor." The Professor would greet visitors and invite the city's most talented musicians to get together and perform for bordello patrons. Jelly Roll Morton, Tony Jackson, Clarence Williams, King Oliver, Professor Longhair and Dr. John were just a few of the musicians who captivated Storyville audiences nightly with vibrant performances.

Storyville boomed; by 1907 there were more than 200 brothels in operation and prostitution was a ten-million-dollar-a-year business. More than 1,500 Ladies worked in Storyville, satisfying every possible whim imaginable. Official maps of Storyville were handed out to men arriving at the New Orleans train station; the district's reputation as a sexual amusement park grew across the nation. Sporting men found themselves overwhelmed with options. According to one estimate, in its heyday Storyville brought in profits of one million dollars a month.

The boom had its downside, not just in the Big Easy but all over the country. Venereal disease was sweeping the nation; more than 40,000 prostitutes a year were dying of syphilis alone. In January of 1917 authorities attempted to clean up Storyville, but it took the advent of World War I to shut the town down. The head of the Department of the Navy ordered every brothel within five miles of a naval base anywhere in the United States closed—not so much for moral reasons, but because venereal disease was seen as just as big a threat to young American males as the Germans. Storyville eventually folded, and all that is left today for tourists to see is a historical sign.

MATA HARI, 1917

Mata Hari, the notorious exotic dancer and courtesan, looking less than fresh on the day she was arrested in 1917, for spying on behalf of Germany during World War I. At her prime, Mata Hari gave promiscuous, Bohemian women everywhere a run for their money. She's quite possibly the original Bond girl! (and the definition of femme fatale).

Condoms:
A Lady's Best Friend

Some researchers claim that the ancient Egyptians, pioneers of so many other sexual innovations, were using condoms as early as 1000 BC. It's difficult to ascertain whether these early condom-like items were used for protection against venereal disease or as a means of birth control (both vital concerns for Ladies). Some historians believe these early sheaths were simply for magical or decorative purposes, or were used as a "cover-up" to maintain modesty.

A popular urban legend claims condoms were invented by a Dr. Condom (sometimes spelled Cundum or Quondam) who served on the court during the reign of Charles II. While historians have debated his existence (and consequent connection with the invention of the sheep-gut sheath that would become the modern-day condom), it is far more likely that the condom received its name from the Latin "condos," which means receptacle.

1500s: There is no doubt that condoms were employed in the 1500s, as evidenced in De morbo gallico, authored by Italian anatomist Gabriello Fallopio (no pun intended). Perhaps because of a widespread outbreak of syphilis, Fallopio recommended a linen sheath as protection against the venereal disease.

1600s: Archeological remains prove that gut condoms existed during the English Civil War. Five of these specimens were found at Dudley Castle.

Condoms began to pop up in literature. The word "condum" first appeared in print in a poem composed around 1706. The journals of famous lover Casanova and James Boswell referred to condoms as "armour," "implements of safety," and the "Redingote Anglaise"—English Riding Coat.

The condoms of old were made through complex methods. A sheep's gut was cut out, soaked, turned inside out and shrunken in an alkaline solution, scraped, exposed to brimstone vapor, washed, blown-up, dried, cut, and then tied with a ribbon.

1800s: *Condoms were well on their way to their modern form. The process of vulcanization, which turns rubber into a strong but elastic material, was developed by Goodyear and Hancock in 1840. This made the condom not only more comfortable but also more practical—leading to a boom in its popularity.*

1861: *The first advertisement for condoms was printed in the New York Times for "Dr. Power's French Preservatives." This historic event was followed closely by the passing of the "Comstock Law" in 1873. This law made the advertising of birth control legal—and its delivery through the United States postal service legal as well.*

1930s: *By the 1930s, liquid latex was manufactured, revolutionizing the condom trade. Sales for these new, more-comfortable-than-ever condoms shot through the roof. The hand-dipping procedure made the production of condoms easier—plus their shelf life was exponentially longer—and millions of condoms were able to be easily mass-produced.*

1957: *The first lubricated condom was launched by the brand Durex.*

In the fifty years since, condoms have come a long way. From their availability in grocery stores and corner markets to their availability in a range of colors, sizes, and textures, condoms have had an interesting journey up to the present, much like the Ladies of the Night.

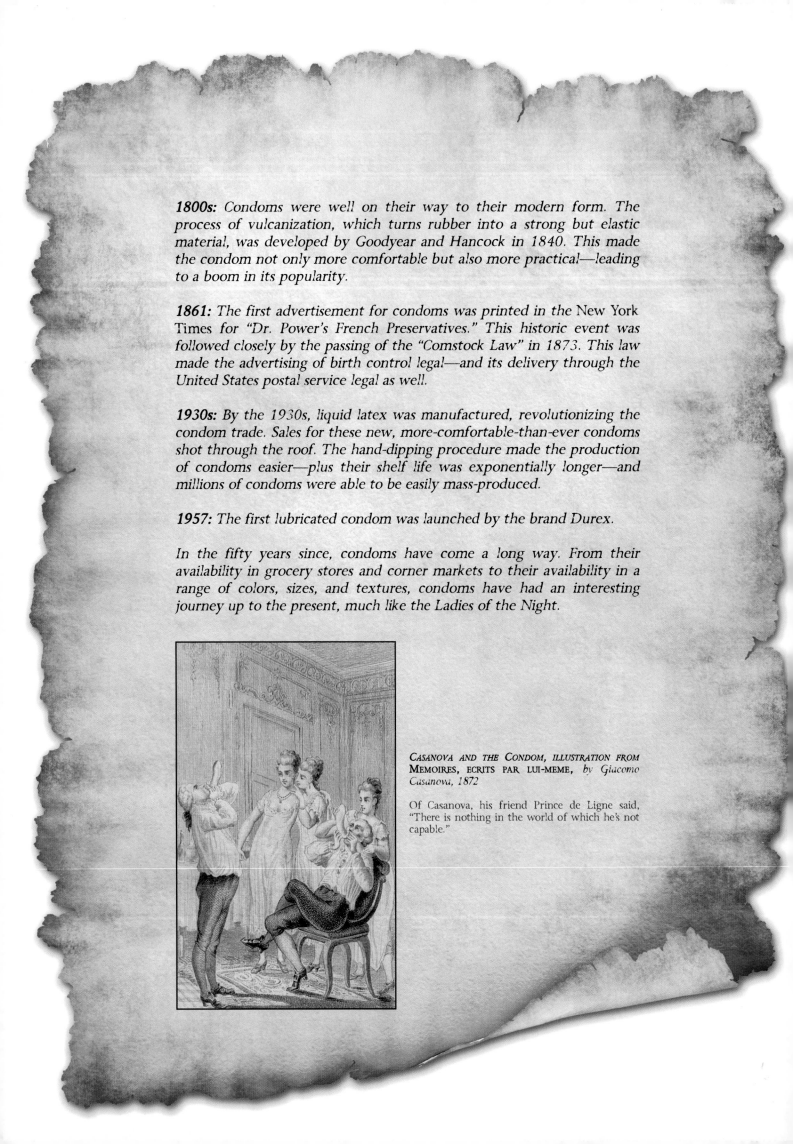

CASANOVA AND THE CONDOM, ILLUSTRATION FROM MEMOIRES, ECRITS PAR LUI-MEME, *by Giacomo Casanova, 1872*

Of Casanova, his friend Prince de Ligne said, "There is nothing in the world of which he's not capable."

CHAPTER SEVENTEEN

The Legal Ladies
of Amsterdam

No book on Ladies of the Night would be complete without a visit to Amsterdam, where the Red Light District has been satisfying men's desires for more than five hundred years. The Dutch have long been recognized for their tolerant stance on drugs and prostitution, making Amsterdam a favorite destination for travelers worldwide to enjoy both pastimes legally. Surprisingly, the official business of sex for sale is not in fact legal in Holland but is officially sanctioned in "toleration zones" in confined areas throughout the country. It remains illegal to sell sex outside such zones. Today an estimated 20,000 full-time official Ladies ply their trade in Holland, though experts believe this number would double if part-timers were included.

Amsterdam has wisely turned its legalized prostitution zones into a major tourist attraction, giving a huge boost to the economy of the country as a whole. The business of sex is an integrated and accepted part of Amsterdam and other cities in Holland. The Ladies themselves are model entrepreneurs. They rent out space and essentially run their own one-person business. Charging 25 to 50 Euros for each twenty-minute "service," they can make up to 500 Euros a day—on which they pay taxes, of course.

By the people, for the people: Democracy and Prostitution

Believe it or not, there have been numerous points in history where brothels and places of prostitution were legalized. Athenian law-maker Solon established the first publicly administered brothel in 549 BC. In fact, Solon discovered rather quickly how profitable a business it was: It created employment opportunities for the lower classes, created tax revenue for the government, and gave an outlet for men to release their sexual desires. In this system, everyone's happy...right?

The most obvious form of prostitution in Amsterdam is on view through the lighted display windows lining the streets of the Red Light District, a picturesque area located in the Old Centre neighborhood. Each window frames a Lady, tapping at passersby to attract attention and tempting them to buy their services. Of course, the Ladies won't tap at just anyone—like all women, they are selective and want the best men. Most of the business happens at night, when the neon lights are out and the tourists and locals alike are ready for action.

Although the windows look small from the street—often prompting the question, "Do they have to do it standing up?"— they are used only to advertise the wares for sale. The real action takes place in the room behind each window, which comes complete with a sink and a bed. Each Lady maintains her own area, just as an American girl might straighten up her office cubicle. She keeps the premises hygienic, insists on the use of condoms and avoids minors.

Ladies of the Night

Police patrol the area with just enough visibility to dissuade most troublemakers. Closed-circuit television cameras monitor street activity, and every window is equipped with an emergency alarm system for the woman to activate if necessary. The vast majority of clients, almost half of whom are locals, have no interest at all in harming a prostitute, but these safeguards give the Ladies a feeling of safety and reassurance.

One misdemeanor that's guaranteed to get a tourist into trouble is taking a photo of a Lady in the window. Snapping pictures is strictly prohibited (although you can find a few online) and will get you marched out of the area by police. Since these Ladies are simply doing their jobs, they'd rather not be treated like zoo animals in cages.

The famous Ladies in the windows of the Red Light District are what Amsterdam is famous for, but a significant part of Holland's prostitution occurs in sex clubs and brothels in every part of the city and countryside. Ranging from bare bones to super-luxurious and pricey, these clubs and brothels find many patrons who prefer a bit more privacy.

Street prostitution is strictly prohibited, though street-walkers, who service the curb-crawling cars and are often associated with drug use and dealing, cannot be completely eradicated. Although a *tippelzone* (tolerated "walking zone") was set up on Theemsweg, complete with private parking stalls, police security, and prostitute support services, the city elected to close it in December 2003, since the Ladies it intended to serve didn't use it much. Some street prostitution does occur in the town center, most notoriously in the area behind Centraal Station.

Amsterdam has its own official Prostitution Information Centre (PIC, which is also slang for "dick" in Dutch...fitting, isn't it?). Founded by a former prostitute named Mariska Majoor in 1994, the Centre is located near the Red Light District and is open to everyone seeking to understand more about prostitutes and the business of sex. PIC is funded through the sale of print information and books related to prostitution, PIC and Red Light souvenirs, and donations. Interested groups can even arrange a lecture session or private walking tour.

Besides the PIC, there are room-rental offices, where women go to rent window-space and the accompanying bedroom to use for prostitution. The men in this office do not arrange sex, but merely act as real estate agents. Ladies have their choice of an eight-, twelve-, or twenty-four-hour window rental. This rental fee includes security—the front desk man also acts as security, keeping an eye on his occupants with a surveillance camera. In addition, he sells supplies: such items as Coca-Cola, lubricants, and condoms (by the case, of course).

The Red Light District, especially at night, is crowded with men walking up and down the street—literally "window shopping." After the woman inside the window and the man outside connect, they talk at the door as she explains her price. Many of these prostitutes are very aggressive at getting the man inside, where the temptation game revs up. A price is agreed upon and paid in advance—before any action takes place.

Dutch law, not pimps, protects prostitutes. If a prostitute is diagnosed with AIDS, she receives a government-subsidized apartment to encourage her to quit the business. This is a good example of a pragmatic Dutch solution to a problem—getting the most dangerous prostitutes off the streets to combat the spread of AIDS.

Are there male prostitutes to service the women tourists? Certainly. Anything your heart desires can be found for sale somewhere in the Red Light District, but an experiment in the 1990s to put male prostitutes in windows proved unsuccessful. There are, however, plenty of "reconstructed women"—gorgeous transvestites who may (or may not) warn customers to ward off any rude surprises. The Red Light District is also home to many gay bars and cinemas, which can be found on the very busy Warmoesstraat.

Actual prostitution aside, there are all kinds of other sex-related stops you can make in Amsterdam. There are numerous

Ladies of the Night

live sex shows, the most famous at the theaters Casa Rosa and infamous Moulin Rouge. For the merely curious, there are lots of peep shows. For the more adventurous there are more interactive shows where audience participation is encouraged—for example, at de Bananenbar (which translates to Banana Bar...I'll leave it to you to imagine why). Videos, magazines, sex aids, toys and condoms can be purchased at one of the many sex shops or sex museums in the area.

The bottom line is that no matter what kind of sex you are seeking, it can be found in Amsterdam. Even better, you can purchase it legally.

AP Images/Peter DeJong

RED LIGHT DISTRICT IN AMSTERDAM

Sexy, scantily clad prostitutes in Amsterdam's notorious
Red Light District beckon male customers to step into their "offices."

Closer to Home:
Legal Ladies in Nevada

If you can't make it to Amsterdam, legal prostitution can be found right here in the USA, in the state of Nevada. Las Vegas is world-famous as Sin City and Ladies are a star attraction...every hotel bar and casino is full of beautiful women trolling for customers. Tourists walking along the Strip are bombarded with flyers advertising the most beautiful escorts in town. A quick walk or one phone call is all it takes to find some company in Las Vegas.

However tolerated and well-established the Las Vegas Ladies are, they aren't officially legal, because prostitution is against the law in Clark County. It IS legal in most other Nevada counties, in the form of brothels, where men gather in the parlor and watch a lineup of Ladies, choose their favorite and negotiate the acts and the price...LEGALLY. There are more than twenty-five legal brothels in Nevada to choose from...including the famous Mustang Ranch, Moonlite Bunny Ranch, and the Chicken House. Hollywood Madam Heidi Fleiss plans to open Heidi's Stud Farm in Crystal, Nevada, a luxury brothel for women only. "What's good for the goose is good for the gander," says Heidi.

AP Images/Debra Reid

This hot-pink complex is the rebuilt Mustang Ranch brothel located just east of Reno. In 2004, construction crews were putting the finishing touches on the Ranch, which was moved from its original location in 1991 due to several federal fraud and racketeering convictions. The Mustang Ranch was Nevada's first licensed brothel in 1971.

CHAPTER EIGHTEEN
Modern-Day Ladies

I recently spent a most enlightening evening with three modern-day Ladies who live in Los Angeles. I was interested in learning more about how they think, because all three of these women made a critical decision at one point in their lives. Something happened, and a light came on.

Tamara, Michelle and Kristie each decided that they were going to enjoy a luxurious lifestyle, one that was going to be financed by men. In other words, they monetized their assets. All three were beautiful, charming, and have very pleasant lives indeed.

What became eminently clear as the night wore on was that these Ladies feel perfectly fine about their choices. They make no apologies to anyone for their lifestyle.

They like themselves.

And they like what they do.

One would presume, so do the men.

I've compiled some highlights from our chats. I hope you enjoy.

GENE SIMMONS

photograph by www.michaelcalasphotography.com

Kristie

I was born and raised in Southern California...and like many women who live here, I'm spoiled rotten.

I started dating when I was fourteen years old and had a serious boyfriend by the time I was fifteen. It was a typical high-school romance. I was a good Catholic girl, and the nuns said I should only have sex after marriage; otherwise it's a sin. But plenty of Catholic girls go ahead and sin anyway, and repent later...and that's what I did, too.

Because after eight or nine months, I could not wait any longer. One Friday night in my boyfriend's bedroom, which had rock posters and *Playboy* centerfolds plastered all over the walls, I decided that this was the night we weren't going to stop. "I'm ready," I told him. He couldn't believe it.... He pulled back from me and said, "Really?" "*Really*," I told him. He was more than ready. Months of pent-up teenage desire were unleashed...we went at each other like animals. We ravaged each other; I was just as eager as he was.

I married this boy as soon as I turned eighteen and we both graduated from high school. He was the only person I'd ever had sex with. We thought we were in love, and couldn't wait to get married and live on our own, away from our parents. Our sex life died as soon as the wedding was over. We went from living at home and having everything handed to us to scraping by on our own in a little apartment. The reality of marriage was tough to take; my illusions vanished within weeks.

My husband and I used to go to the beach all the time. After we got married I really started to pay attention to all the Barbie-doll girls getting out of convertible Ferraris, accompanied by older, suntanned guys with spiky hair and Rolex watches. I knew I was just as pretty as any one of them.... I was eighteen years old, with long blond hair and a perfect body. I was a bored and restless newlywed and soon came to a life-changing decision:

I want to be that girl. That's why my marriage only lasted six months. My eighteen-year-old husband was simply not able to provide the lifestyle I thought should be mine.

I loved my husband, but I was not about to live such an unglamorous existence when there was so much more out there. I cut my losses and left. I was determined to be *that girl*... loading bags from Barney's and Saks Fifth Avenue and Neiman Marcus into my Aston Martin on Rodeo Drive. And it didn't take long.

Some girlfriends and I went to a boxing match, and a very tall man, at least six-foot-seven, approached me. "Hey, baby," he said, grabbing my hand. "Please tell me you're not married."

That was my introduction to a whole new life. This new man was a professional basketball player, and he was crazy about me. In three months I had a new Mercedes; within a year he had put a sizeable down payment on a condo in Beverly Hills. His accountant transferred money into my bank account every month, and if I needed cash, I just asked. I got a gold Amex card with my own name on it, and I shopped to my heart's content. We spent a blissful three years together...three years that ruined me for ninety percent of the male population.

The basketball player and I parted amicably after three years, when he got traded to a team on the East Coast; neither of us were the kind for a long-distance relationship. I was in L.A., twenty-one years old, and there were plenty of rich men around. I've maintained that lifestyle ever since...with the help of quite a few generous gentlemen.

The one thing I don't do is play around with married men. I don't have to; there are plenty who are divorced or still playing the field. I wouldn't want anyone to sleep with my husband, so I don't do it to anyone else. I fell in love, once, with a very well-known billionaire publisher...who adored me, I thought. Chanel bags, Bulgari jewelry, skiing trips...life was perfect for eight months, until a girlfriend of mine told me he was hitting on her, always trying to get her number. I was crushed.... The next time he came over to my house I threw that Bulgari necklace in his

Ladies of the Night

face and screamed, "Get out!" Later, after I'd calmed down, I realized that was a dumb financial move. At least I should have kept the gifts! I won't make that mistake again.

I'm not the kind of woman a man can pick up in a club, or call when he's in town for the weekend. I'm all about long-term relationships...I demand to be treated as a valued girlfriend. What I do isn't a job; it's maintaining my lifestyle. I am well-known in Los Angeles; I sit at my regular table at Spago on Saturday nights and Monday evenings at Mr. Chow's. A conventional relationship where the woman works a job, raises the kids, and saves her pennies to shop at Target is just beyond the limits of my imagination.

I don't know if I'll ever get married.... I've been engaged several times, but I get nervous as the date approaches. I start to feel trapped and hemmed in and can't follow through. I don't need to get married, because I'm now independently wealthy.... I've invested wisely over the years. I'm now at the point where I don't even need a man.... I can spoil myself.

But I love men...the richer the better. There's an attitude that wealthy men exude that just turns me on. It's that unmistakable air of self-confidence and power. I can spot a millionaire or billionaire anywhere.... They wear that certain attitude on their sleeve, just like their $250,000 watches.

What I do is simply live the L.A. life. It's the way every one of my friends lives...whether they're dating, living with, married to, separated from, or divorced from their own mogul or rock star. I'm having fun...my life is all about leisure and pleasure. You only live once...why not do it wearing Christian Dior and carrying a Chanel bag?

What are my choices? To work as hard as I can, sacrifice any personal life, and still lose out to a man when it comes time for a promotion? That's simply a fact of life; men dominate the business world. I've achieved great success...and I did it my way.

Bottom line? If you have your own heliport and private jet, and are ready to whisk me away to my dream destination, I'd love to meet you. Believe me, I'm worth it.

GENE SIMMONS

photograph by www.michaelcalasphotography.com

Michelle

Men enjoy the kill, but what they really love is the chase. A woman's power lies in prolonging the hunt. It's a game: how long can you drag the relationship out before giving in? Let's face it, once a woman "gives in," she's no longer as fascinating and mysterious. This is simply the way of the world; an exchange exists between men and women, and anyone who denies that is simply fooling herself.

It all seems very clear-cut to me, perhaps because I have very few illusions. I was raised in a nudist colony in Canada. My first sexual experience was with another girl at the age of nine, and I lost my virginity to a boyfriend at fourteen. After that, all bets were off, so I guess you could say I've always been quite open-minded.

I'm all grown up now and live in L.A., where I'm an actress and a painter. I've always liked men, and they've always liked me. I meet them everywhere, all the time, when I'm out and about in Hollywood clubs or restaurants in Beverly Hills. My personal weakness is for bad-boy musicians…but I've been there and done that, and I can't say it got me anywhere. Money is most definitely an important factor in my relationships…because the more options a man has, the more appealing he is in every way. A hot guy in a VW van isn't going to do it for me anymore. A Bentley, on the other hand, is very inviting.

Nowadays I look for the strong, successful type. I like a man who knows what he wants and goes after it. Frequently, what they want is me. I'm very friendly and open and approachable, but I'm also very selective. If I meet an attractive man at a club who asks me to come back to his hotel room that night, it's clear they're only looking for a one-night stand. And I'm not into that. I understand it, I'm fine with it, but I'm not that kind of a girl. I'm a little old-fashioned…I like to be courted. A gentleman should be happy to pay for a woman's time and company.

So a man has to take me on a few dates before anything physical happens. There will most definitely be a trip so I can see how we get along...to a destination like Paris, Bali or Hawaii. There will be long dinners and nice jewelry and plenty of spoiling before I fulfill his fantasies...and I always come through in that department. I'm a very imaginative lover...anything goes, from toys to domination to other women. I'm well worth the wait; I never disappoint.

All of this is unspoken, by the way. I never have to spell out what I want to a man in so many words. If I have to ask a man to buy me something, take me somewhere, or pursue him in any way, he's not the right one for me. I move on immediately. I'm going to get what I want, and be treated well along the way, and there are plenty of men willing to accommodate my wishes. Women are beautiful goddesses, and men should be pleased to pay to spend time with us.

This attitude really crystallized when I was eighteen years old and went to Paris to visit a girlfriend. She had an older French lover, who flew us to England on his private jet to vacation at his estate there. He showered us both with clothes, jewelry and cash. He treated my girlfriend very well; he was doting and respectful. I was just out of high school, dating musicians—I'd never seen a relationship like this before. Once I got a taste of this life, I saw no reason to ever live any other way. *What are you doing?* I asked myself on the plane ride home. *You can live this way too!* And so I have, ever since.

There have been quite a few men since that time who were willing to keep me in the manner to which I quickly became accustomed. I always ask if a man is married...but I'm aware that many don't tell the truth on this subject. It's not necessarily a dealbreaker in any case. I've dated the occasional woman, too...very successful and well-off ladies. You would think it would be easier to have a relationship with another woman, but I soon learned that they can be just as jealous and possessive as any man.

These days I'm having a great time and living a wonderful lifestyle. I don't care what society or any other women might think of me, because they don't have to pay my bills or live my life. Maybe someday I'll settle down; if I meet the "right" man, whatever that means. I don't waste my energy worrying about that—I am enjoying my life very much just the way it is.

If you want me, you need to bring plenty to the table. I expect dinners, trips, flowers, jewelry and plenty of romance and attention. I'm worth it.

Tamara

I strongly believe that a woman should be free to pursue whatever lifestyle she chooses. I've modeled and acted part-time all my adult life, and I could certainly see myself working full-time, but I've never had to. Men have always taken care of me. I'm not ashamed of that fact, but I'm wearing a mask because society often judges women like me harshly. Most women are threatened by my appearance right off the bat and not inclined to like me. If everyone knew all about the things I've done, the world would look at me differently…even though secretly I believe those who judge me are envious of my lifestyle.

Beautiful women have power…a fact I became aware of when I was about fifteen and my breasts appeared overnight. I started wearing makeup too, and the boys paid lots of attention to me from that time on. In high school I dated our star football player, but when I met the star quarterback from the rival high school across town I decided to lose my virginity to him. He was much better-looking.

I can't say it was a great experience…for one thing, it was quite painful. We did the deed in his bedroom, and his parents

photograph by www.michaelcalasphotography.com

came home and caught us naked in his bed together. I had to run into the bathroom, put on my clothes and leave. It was very embarrassing…and even though I really liked him, I never saw him again. He had scored…all he wanted from me was sex.

I was eighteen years old and living with my parents in Las Vegas when a girlfriend of mine went for a job interview as a chauffeur. The forty-two-year-old man who hired her to drive him around took a liking to me and asked me out. He was my first millionaire: limos, trips, gifts, cash…I loved every minute of it. We dated for almost a year…until he was sent to prison on drug-related charges. That was the end of him…but I was hooked on the lifestyle.

Since then there have probably been twenty or more millionaires in my life. At the age of twenty-three, I met a Hollywood star in the VIP room of a nightclub in Beverly Hills. He asked me to dance, took my number, sent me flowers the next day, and we dated for more than a year. He, too, took good care of me…lavishing me with vacations and jewelry. He was sixty-three years old but I didn't mind a bit.… I liked older men, and he was still very handsome.

After that there was no chance of me ever dating the guy who works for the sanitation department and drives a beat-up car. I am accustomed to nice things and a certain lifestyle. The more money a man makes, the more attractive he becomes; that's just a fact of life. I love men, and I love sex, so I might have sex just with a "regular" guy…but that's purely for fun…and it stays our little secret. The millionaire doesn't know about him. Ever.

I keep all the men I've dated very happy sexually. Some men like the little-girl act, which I'm very good at; others need lots of stimulation. I've brought a girlfriend into the picture a few times for a threesome, just to spice things up…I make sure they're satisfied.

The richest man I ever dated was a billionaire, and we had a great time together. He was a real high roller; we went to Vegas all the time and lived the high life. Around that time I met an agent in L.A. with a specialty. To put it bluntly, she supplied women for the Sultan of Brunei. She took pictures of me, similar to modeling photos, and put them in a book along with those of lots of other gorgeous girls from L.A. She then flew to London to meet with the Sultan's representative, who picked from the various photos. I was among those chosen to fly to Brunei to entertain the Sultan and his brother.

I flew from L.A. to Brunei first class on a commercial airline, along with six other beautiful girls. We arrived to encounter a complete harem. There were at least fifty girls staying on the grounds of the Sports Palace, every nationality imaginable. Thai, Canadian, Spanish, English, Americans...they came and went and rotated all the time.

All that was required of us was to attend a party every night. The girls were on the menu, and the Sultan's brother chose one or another each night. During the day we worked out, sat by the pool, watched movies...it got quite boring, actually. I spent a lot of time on the phone with my mother—who was all for this trip, by the way. Because the financial rewards were incredible.

I was paid $3,000 a day just to be available to mingle at night. On my birthday I was given $70,000 cash, just as a gift. And all the girls were given Cartier or Rolex watches and a matching set of jewelry from Harry Winston. In six months, I made a half-million dollars; if you add in the value of the jewelry I would estimate I cleared $700,000. And the most incredible part was that I never had sex. Certainly I understood that was part of the deal; and I would have done it, but I was never chosen. My roommate was and was given an additional $100,000 bonus.

I eventually grew so bored that I asked to leave Brunei... and looking back now, I regret it. If I was asked to return right now, I'd do it in a heartbeat.

Money makes everybody happy...I'll just come right out and admit it. When I'm at a club and a Rolls-Royce pulls up outside, my heart starts to beat a little faster. I'm nobody's one-night stand...I'm the companion to millionaires and billionaires. I love my lifestyle, and I intend to keep on living it. I was married to a rich man once, briefly, and I'd love to get married again...but multi-millionaires only, please!

Jets, gems, cash...and, ideally, love...that's what it takes to make me happy. And I'm worth it.

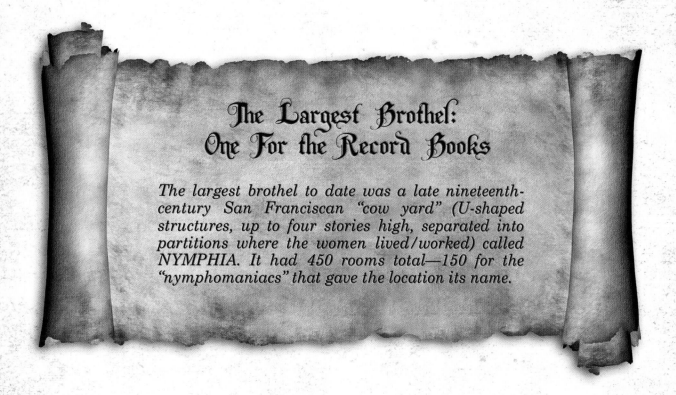

The Largest Brothel: One For the Record Books

The largest brothel to date was a late nineteenth-century San Franciscan "cow yard" (U-shaped structures, up to four stories high, separated into partitions where the women lived/worked) called NYMPHIA. It had 450 rooms total—150 for the "nymphomaniacs" that gave the location its name.

Famous Madams

AP Images/Dave Pickoff

LYNN REDGRAVE applies makeup in preparation for the New York City filming of *The Happy Hooker* (1974), based on the book by Xaviera Hollander.

Ladies of the Night have been with us throughout history. And some of them were entrepreneurs. These "special Ladies" realized that they could make more money by "spreading the risk" instead of only betting on themselves.

By the twentieth century (in Western culture, at least) the Lady of the Night was frowned upon. America was no longer the "Wild West" of less than a hundred years earlier. This was a more cultured society...or that's what people liked to believe. The truth is, business as usual continued.

What happened next was an "awakening" in some Ladies.

The birth of the Pill in the sixties enabled women to start making some real decisions about their own sexuality. Society would no longer dictate to women when, where or how they would have sex. Marriage, though still highly respected, was no longer the only option open to them. Pre-marital sex became the norm. Abstinence, the exception.

Society and pop culture started reflecting the changing social mores in song, literature and movies. Free love, hippies, rock and roll...all contributed to the phenomenon that was about to happen: "THE ROCK STAR MADAM!"

She was flamboyant. She was entrepreneurial—upon retiring from active work, she decided to take what she knew about the business and manage the careers of others instead of taking customers herself. And she became famous.

In modern times, the first legendary contemporary Madam lived in New York in the 1970s. Her name was **Xaviera Hollander**, and she was known as The Happy Hooker.

The young secretary at the Dutch consulate in Manhattan was disenchanted with her job and its low pay. "Why are you giving it away?" she was asked one day. "You are sitting on a gold mine!" That was all it took. Soon the pretty blond with the exotic accent was a high-class call girl, seeing seven or eight clients a day and charging $1,000 for each appointment.

AP Images/Ed Bailey

Here the *MAYFLOWER MADAM*, Sydney Biddle Barrows, speaks at a press conference in New York City in 1985, one month after she pleaded guilty to promoting prostitution.

A year later, Xaviera was doing so well that she decided to open her own brothel. She purchased the "black book" of a retiring madam and printed up business cards with a number to call "when you want to get laid." She ran her business out of a Manhattan high-rise with a number of other sex-related companies in the building, fighting off fierce competition both in her own building and all over the city. Busted by the New York police, she was arrested and forced to leave the country. But before she departed for her hometown of Amsterdam, she wrote the blockbuster bestseller The Happy Hooker.

Sydney Biddle Barrows was an unlikely madam: she came from a prominent society family in Philadelphia, the Biddles, who traced their lineage all the way back to the Mayflower. Sydney graduated from the Fashion Institute of Technology, but after being introduced to the world of high-class prostitution during a chance encounter in the unemployment line, she decided her best bet was a different kind of business.

Her agency, Cachet, was the perfect merger of business and sex in 1980s New York City. Sydney catered to a very high-end clientele and was known for her beautiful girls and discreet, elegant service. Cachet was a million-dollar-a-year operation, until her Upper West Side headquarters was raided

AP Photo/Melbourne Age/Angela Wylie

HEIDI DOES AUSTRALIA
Heidi Fleiss, one of the most infamous madams in recent memory, is photographed at the Melbourne, Australia Stock Exchange in 2003 after helping to launch the country's first publicly traded brothel. Heidi has been well-schooled in the business world, especially after her 1997 arrest for pandering and tax evasion.

by police. She eventually turned herself into the police, pleaded guilty to promoting prostitution and paid a $5,000 fine. Her best-selling book, The Mayflower Madam, was made into a television movie starring Candice Bergen.

Ten years later on the West Coast, **Heidi Fleiss**, the daughter of a prominent pediatrician, became notorious worldwide as the Hollywood Madam. After a brief apprenticeship with an older Madam, she overtook her mentor and ran her own high-end call-girl ring out of Los Angeles throughout the nineties. Her girls were gorgeous, her clients rich and famous, and her little black book held the biggest names in Hollywood. Just a few years after dropping out of high school, she became the most influential Madam in the world.

"I took the oldest profession on earth and did it better than anyone on earth," she told CNN. "Alexander the Great conquered the world at 32. I conquered it at 22."

The law came down hard on Heidi; she was eventually arrested after an undercover operation and served nearly two years in prison for tax evasion and pandering. Her harsh sentence outraged many; she was severely punished for a seemingly victimless crime, while all of her clients got off scot-free. These days she's planning a return to her old profession, but this time legally. Heidi's Stud Farm, a brothel selling the services of MEN, caters to women only. It is scheduled to open soon in Nevada.

Conclusion

FINALLY, HERE'S THE BIG IDEA:

It may be time to legalize "The Trade."

This doesn't mean that I plan to start a personal campaign, or want to engage in debates with religious, social or ethical groups. I actually have no axe to grind either way. Pragmatism may be the deciding factor here.

No matter how hard governments try to ban Ladies of the Night from advertising their wares and charging those willing to pay for the pleasures thereof—the results have been minimal. Translation: You can't stop it.

No one has ever been able to stop the Trade, simply because it tends to be something the male of the species continues to want: time after time, century after century, for as long as we have been in existence. My sense is, it will always be here.

Just like drinking. Almost everywhere in the world, since the dawn of civilization, people have wanted to drink alcohol. Lots of it. Some governments (like those in some of today's Islamic countries) ban alcohol consumption of any kind. I doubt, however, if this can ever be successfully enforced.

America too, once tried to ban drinking. It was called Prohibition, and it existed in the 1920s. But not for long. An underground criminal empire sprouted up overnight because the government didn't allow its people to do something they wanted to do. So the people turned elsewhere to satisfy their demand. The result? The birth of America's nationwide criminal organizations.

Once Prohibition was repealed and drinking became legal again, alcohol as part of the criminal trade almost entirely ceased to be a factor. The government took over. They taxed the alcohol industry and made money doing it. Lots of it. They set guidelines regarding quality, truth in advertising and other issues, and saved the money it cost to wage war on alcohol and those who wanted to drink it.

I personally have never been drunk. I also never engage in "social drinking." It simply doesn't appeal to me, though I don't condemn or judge others who enjoy it. In cultures worldwide, including many European countries, there is a Culture of Wine (translation: Booze Appreciation—i.e., they like the taste and the effect it has on them). "Spirits," they call them. "Booze," I call it. Whatever it's called, people want it, so it exists. And it will continue to exist, no matter who tries to stop it.

Older than drinking is the Trade. It predates civilization, language, currency...well, almost everything. And trying to stop it seems a futile, if not impossible task. All over the world, the Trade exists and continues to do well. And that's because men want it to exist.

For the record, I have never hired the services of a Lady of the Night.

If I ever did, she would have to pay me.

The reason I was interested in doing this book was that in a free society such as ours, shouldn't we be able to have as many choices as we want? Both at work and in our private lives?

Isn't a Lady of the Night simply empowering herself and making her own decisions, regardless of what society says?

Ladies of the Night

Isn't what goes on behind closed doors between two or more consenting adults a matter of privacy?

Should Government, Religion and Society have a say in everything we do?

Do we all have to conform to someone else's view of what makes us happy?

Shouldn't we legalize the Trade once and for all?

Because whether we do or not, it will continue to exist.

It always has.

It always will.

Thank you

A special thank you to the publisher, Michael Viner at Phoenix Books, Julie McCarron, Alina Poniewaz and for extraordinary design work, thank you Sonia.